Perception

2nd Edition

Understanding Human Connectivity
through the DISC Behavioral Model

Editing: K. J. Green

Cover Image: Fotolia
All Manuscript Images: Creative Commons

This publication is sold with the understanding that neither the publisher nor the author is engaged in rendering legal or professional services. If legal or policy advice is prudent, the reader should seek competent assistance in that area.

ISBN: 978-0-9817-1167-6

Published by:
Glocal Press
Williamsburg, Virginia
Contact: jeff.green@cpleinternational.org

Library of Congress Control Number: 2022920502

In *Perception*, Dr. Jeff Green has provided a succinct and extremely understandable description of one of the most popular behavioral profiling models in use today. Particularly insightful are the various scenarios he uses to enhance the reader's understanding of how DISC can be applied to know oneself and equally important, to improve communication. A must read for those intent on improving both their emotional and social intelligence.

—Dr. Neil Moore
President/CEO
TalMar Training and Consulting

In *Perception*, Dr. Green explains the DISC model in a fun and colloquial way, providing each of us with additional tools to increase our understanding of conflict management and show us a path to achieving more effective communications. With communication being such a vital part of our daily lives, DISC provides a tremendous insight into understanding and improving one's own personal skills as well as improving the overall lines of communication with the citizens we serve. *Perception* will be a permanent reference on my desk.

—Andrea Buchanan, CFO, IPSLEI
Chief Deputy Fire Marshal
Alexandria (Virginia) Fire Department

Perception is a must read for those in leadership positions or really everyone hoping to expand their influence and reach with others. We all have unique ways of viewing and responding to the world around us. However, through the DISC model, we can learn certain patterns within our behaviors that can lead to stronger understandings of one another, better communications at any level, reduced tension and conflict, and increased tolerance—all requisite characteristics of successful people and organizations. Dr. Green presents the DISC model with the expertise of a long-time scholar and DISC practitioner but in a relaxed and easy to understand way as if we are sitting around a table drinking a cup of coffee. Dr. Green has given us *Perception* as a practical guide leading us forward.

—R. Allen Brandon
Director
York County (South Carolina) Dept. of Public Safety
Communications Center

In *Perception,* Dr. Green breaks down the DISC model to make its methodology and use easy to understand and apply. We see how others react and behave in their own surroundings as well as how we may behave in those same situations in everyday life. A refreshing read on a topic often taken too deep for the everyday person.

—Scott Grafton
Owner
Iron-Bound Gym (IBG)
Williamsburg, Virginia

Dr. Green's inimitable, thought-provoking book has integrated the timeless benefits of DISC awareness with the inherent human need for emotional and cognitive connectivity. This transcendent concept is the catalyst for a relationship renaissance improving family dynamics, business operations, and government service and accountability. Jeff's interpersonal emphasis makes *Perception* powerful and deeply meaningful.

—Les Kachurek
Chief of Police (ret)
Northern Kentucky University
Alfred State University

Dr. Jeff Green has made psychological theory and the DISC Model accessible and applicable. He uses entertaining and familiar examples to clearly illustrate how people can experience the same events very differently because of their unique tendencies and perspectives. We all can benefit from taking time to understand our own tendencies as well as those of others around us. Dr. Green articulately guides his readers to help them develop an understanding of themselves and others that can lead to more effective communication across all contexts of their lives.

—Nicole Guajardo, PhD
Professor of Psychology
Dean
College of Natural and Behavioral Sciences
Christopher Newport University

With *Perception*, Jeff has given the leader an advantage by clearing up the mysteries of personality as it relates to the leader/follower relationship. Characteristics that were once inhibitors to leadership can become advantages to those who understand and use these concepts. Regardless of the discipline, the best leaders attempt to make personal and emotional connections with their constituents. They try to understand and appreciate the needs, motives, and aspirations of those who look to them for leadership. At the heart of our personality lies a realm of emotions and motivation waiting to be called to action. Those who use the lessons from *Perception* will become more impactful and effective leaders regardless of their position or field of practice.

—David L. Allen, MPA
Allen Solutions LLC
Charlotte, North Carolina

Perception

2nd Edition

Understanding Human Connectivity
through the DISC Behavioral Model

Jeffrey L. Green, PhD

Glocal Press
Williamsburg, Virginia

Between stimulus and response there is a space.
In that space is our power to choose our response.
In our response lies our growth and our freedom.

Viktor Frankl, M.D.

CONTENTS

FOREWORD

Perception, by my good friend Dr. Jeff Green, is a fantastic primer to providing clear direction for your journey through the often-confusing challenge of self-discovery and self-development with the end goal of delivering RESULTS with CONFIDENCE in everything you do.

A student asked his teacher, "Master, what is happiness?" The master replied graciously, "Grandfather die, father die, son die." The stunned student blurted, "Master, how can such unspeakable tragedy be happiness?" The answer: "Because it is the Natural order of things." This is the epitome of perspective; learn to *see* the real meaning in everything especially with human interaction whether you are considering a thought, a word, or a deed. Perception largely determines how we function in the world.

One of the quintessential questions of philosophers, pundits, and poets centers on perspective. The Oriental Ancients tell us to "learn the two-fold gaze of sight and perception." Sight, what meets the eye, is weak. Perception, what it all really means, is strong; it gives meaning to what we sense. Perceiving is a skill that develops only with long and consistent study. The Ancients call it "practice." Practice needs to begin early and continue throughout life. One insight leads to the clearer view of two more and so on; thus, we grow. Perception is also perspective. It is learning about self. For that I turn again to Oriental wisdom by way of a brief introduction to hopefully what becomes a lifelong pursuit.

Miyamoto Musashi, Japan's most famous samurai, outlined his Way, which is one of the most famous treatises on how to perceive, thus how to live life (1974, p. 49). His wisdom has themes that occupied the ancients for many centuries and concern us still today.

- *Do not think dishonestly.* It is no coincidence the Master begins with honesty. He knew that without knowing right from wrong and doing right, not much good can come of the potential in life. This is the basis of living the Good Life with happiness at stake.
- *The Way is in training.* Practice worthy pursuits vigorously. This also means to choose wisely what we do because doing something essential and well usually takes a lifetime.
- *Become acquainted with every art.* This is becoming a well-rounded person. Be informed. Learn to love learning. Learn the meaning of all you learn. Then apply what you learn. Nothing happens without practiced action.
- *Know the ways of all professions.* Every way of making a living has lessons for how to conduct a life.
- *Distinguish between gain and loss in world matters.* Simply, money, power, and position are not everything, especially if they are misused. The respect of respectable people, in the end, matters.
- *Perceive those things which cannot be seen.* There is always hidden meaning, which makes all the difference from the mundane to the profound.
- *Pay attention even to trifles.* Attention to the correct details matters.
- *Do nothing which is of no use.* Life is not a dry run. Time well used is what makes life accomplished and meaningful.

Perception is only part of living well, but it is a basic part. Doing life well is really the process of self-discovery—self-awareness, self-evaluation and self-motivation. It is a cycle of "...growing, knowing, discovering, remembering (Cicero, 2012, p. 33)" and growing again.

BRAVO Jeff!

Mitch Javidi, PhD

Chancellor, National Command & Staff College
Honorary Member of US Army Special Command

ACKNOWLEDGMENT

Writing a book takes a great deal of hard work, effort, and sacrifice from many different people. I first want to than my wife and children. Writing and researching certainly takes time away from other endeavors. But more importantly, I want to thank them for being great partners along the way. My children grew up learning the language of DISC. Then in recent years, my new children (my daughter and son got married) were immersed in language and power of DISC. My family could have written this book just as easily as me. They have humored me with hearing my thoughts and reading these pages over and over again, particularly with this second edition. They offered nuanced insights and criticisms to make me and the book better. Thank you, Kathy, Alexandra & Daniel, and Justin & Katey for your thoughts, shared enthusiasm, and unyielding support.

I am forever indebted to the many friends and colleagues over the years who provided their guidance and expertise in this journey. Thank you to Dr. David Corderman and Dr. Tim Turner, who first exposed me to the DISC model and to Charles Robb, Mike McAuliffe, Jack Cantalupo, Steve Smith, Paul Bertrand and so many others who I taught the model with side by side over many, many years at the FBI Academy. A special thank you to David Allen and Tim Plotts. You not only are subject matter experts and world-class instructors - you listened, critiqued, and made this book better all along the way.

I also would like to thank the many prominent contributors who took the time to review Perception and offer their praise for the cover and inside pages. I owe a special debt and gratitude to Dr. Mitch Javidi, Chancellor of the National Command & Staff College, for evaluating the manuscript and taking the time to author such an insightful foreword.

Finally, I want to thank the countless students who have engaged with me in the classroom for so many years. Without your passion, engagement, sharp questions, and subsequent stories about how the model changed your lives at home and work, this book never would have been written.

MAKING SENSE OF OUR WORLD 1

All of us are interested in finding out more about ourselves and others. Our natural curiosity about the world clearly applies to our role in it and the ways we respond to it. As highlighted by the title of this book (Perception), the lens through which we view our environment and subsequently respond to it, is informed by our perceptions. As Stephen Covey aptly offered, "We see the world not as it is, but as we are."

> *"Know thyself" was the inscription over the Oracle at Delphi. And it is still the most difficult task any of us face. But until you truly know yourself, strengths and weaknesses, know what you want to do and why you want to do it, you cannot succeed in any but the most superficial sense of the word.*
>
> —Warren Bennis

DISC is a behavioral model developed by Dr. William Marston in the 1920s intended to identify and categorize how people respond to their environment. The actual DISC assessment or instrument was not developed until after his death decades later. The instruments (they come in all sizes and formats) are not a measure of one's skills, nor are they all-encompassing personality instruments. Many people refer to DISC as a personality assessment, but DISC assesses only one component of personality – our observable, surface-level responses to the world.

It is easy to confuse personality with behavior. After all, behavior is clearly informed by personality. Personality tests, such as the Myers-Briggs Type Indicator (MBTI) or Minnesota Multiphasic Personality Inventory (MMPI), describe how people think, sense, and feel. These characteristics generally do not significantly change over time. The DISC model acknowledges the innate elements of human behavior, such as those measured by the MBTI, while recognizing the influence of the environment. The DISC model shows one's natural or intrinsic behavioral style and one's learned or adapted behavioral style. The distinction may appear subtle; however, the implication is significant. While innate traits will change little over time, behavioral style can be fluid. Indeed, our behavior should be fluid based on the needs of the situation. Thus, the strength of DISC rests not only in its ability to measure and categorize observable behaviors and emotions but also in its ability to provide the necessary information for individuals to exercise more flexibility in a variety of situations.

The text's journey introduces the historical foundations of the DISC model followed by a focus on the benefits and potential dangers or misuses of the model. Before providing any specificity on the model, we move to the validated behavioral self-assessment. Decades of experience indicate an understanding of the model prior to completing the assessment can impact how participants respond. We then move to an explanation of your specific profile. Looking in the mirror is one of the most valuable aspects of the model. From here the text takes a deeper dive into the different dimensions of human behavior and the theoretical underpinnings of the model with fun, real-life examples illustrating the model and theory. The concluding chapters focus on recognizing other people's behavioral preferences and then actionizing better relationships with this understanding. We begin with a brief exploration of the title of the book, *Perception*.

HOW WE PERCEIVE

Seeing is believing, right? Well, I think so. Surely, most people trust their own eyes. The problem is that believing something does not make it true. We have an interesting duality happening within our internal belief systems. On the one side of this Trust coin, when we see something, we then believe it to exist exactly as we see it. I see a black and blue dress, so I assume (incorrectly) that everyone sees the dress as black and blue. Even if we can agree on the physical nature of what we see, how we experience it will vary among each of us. I see the delivery truck pass my neighbor's house and stop in front of mine. I'm excited because I have been impatiently waiting on something I have wanted for quite a while. My neighbor sees the same event – the delivery truck pulling up to my house. Yet, he is frustrated because he has been expecting an important package, which obviously is not coming today. We saw the same thing but *perceived* it in very different ways. What we think is an objective reality often is not. How we perceive everything is unique to each of us.

On the other side of the coin, *until* we do see something, we have difficulty believing it really exists. There was a person in an association I belonged to many years ago who was rumored to be okay if he was on his medications. But when off his meds, he would explode for unexplainable reasons at the most inappropriate times. I had not seen this side of him. He was always kind and professional around me. Then a few years later, I saw the explosion. Until that occasion, it is fair to say I really did not believe the rumors. I trusted my other friends' words and assumptions, but human nature is that until we see something for ourselves, particularly if it stands in opposition to what we have seen, we just have difficulty believing it. Once I saw the meltdown, I was a believer.

Our brains will reject perfectly feasible information simply because it has negative implications for our beliefs. Likewise, it will tend to enthusiastically accept information with positive implications even if that information is inaccurate. The irony here is powerful. This dichotomy of trust can lead to completely incorrect assumptions, which may then lead to erroneous or inappropriate decisions, judgments, behaviors, and responses to the world and people around us.

OUR LYING (OR AT LEAST MISLEADING) EYES

Almost two and a half centuries ago, Aristotle first numbered the senses in his work *De Anima*: Sight, hearing, smell, taste, and touch. However, neurologists today would count at least nine senses – the big five plus thermoception - the sense of heat; nociception - pain; equilibrioception - balance; and proprioception - body awareness (close your eyes and touch your nose). Eco-psychologist Michael Cohen puts the number of senses at 54 including such additional sensations as temperature, gravity, air, motion, hunger, and mental distress.

Whatever the real number, we depend on our senses to see the world around us. Yet just because we see or hear something does not mean it exists in the way we see or hear it. We may look up on a sunny day and see a clear blue sky. Most of us there will agree the sky is blue. But rest assured we all are not seeing, experiencing the same blue. I may be seeing something more akin to your purple, and you may be seeing something more akin to my green. Indeed, color does not even exist as an object reality. Color is an individual perception of energy and wavelengths of light that our eyes see. We have known since Isaac

Newton's experiments with light and color in the late 1600s that our eyes sense light, which consists of many waves with varying lengths. Most objects do not make light themselves. Instead, light from the sun or man-made lights, for example, strikes them. Depending on the object, some wavelengths will be reflected, while others will be absorbed. When we look at an object, our eyes see the waves of light that have bounced off. And this happens extremely fast because light moves so fast.

Our eyes allow our brains to see what is out in the world, but our eyes do not provide meaning to what we see. So, while our eyes clearly play a key role in bringing color to existence, they need help. Enter our brains, particularly our cerebral cortex. Whether through our eyes or the many other senses we have both known and unknown, data is brought to the brain and then interpreted into something we can understand. We may think we see the world objectively (a blue sky in this case), but that thinking would be incorrect. As you can imagine, a lot can go wrong in the interpretation.

Remember *The Dress* in February 2015. It was an Internet phenomenon that went viral on the global stage unlike anything seen before. And it absolutely upended the notion that we have a full understanding of how color vision works. If you recall, a picture of a dress, taken from a cell phone, was captioned with "What Color Is the Dress – Blue and Black or White and Gold?" The world went nuts! Why? Because about 40 percent saw blue and black, about 40 percent saw white and gold, and the rest saw varying shades of brown and blue or no color whatsoever. Some even saw both. *The Dress* revealed stunning individual differences in color perception. Yet, I would suggest it revealed stunning individual differences across every aspect of our perceptions of our world and ourselves.

The Dress did not only baffle the masses. Scientists who study the visual system equally were bewildered by the illusion. Extensive research has been conducted regarding **figures** with nuanced uncertainty (e.g., face/vase, duck/rabbit) that has helped scientists reveal principles of visual perception, but this color illusion was vastly more unique. Notions and ideas of explanation abounded within days of The Dress. Yet, most were quickly debunked. No one truly knew why some people saw blue and black and others white and gold. We arguably still do not fully understand it today.

Remember that color is the wavelength or frequency at which light bounces off a surface. However, the dress reflects the same amount of light for everyone, so the answer to the mystery rests in something that comes after the reception of the data. It must be in the interpretation of the data by the brain. According to neuroscientist and psychologist Pascal Wallisch, color is "something we make up in our heads." Many influences impact the way we interpret different hues from light to context. One such contextual influence is "the viewing history of the individual observer." Our perceptions of our world, color in this case, are at least in part based on our memories and experiences with similar engagements. The photo of the dress contained a lot of uncertainty in terms of lighting conditions. Was it taken inside or outside? Was the dress illuminated from the front or the back? It is well-established that in situations like this where the brain faces profound uncertainty, it unapologetically fills in the spaces by making assumptions. Usually, its assumptions are based on what it has most frequently encountered in the past.

Look at the following optical illusion. Because our brains are overwhelmed by contrasting stimuli and uncertainty, our minds begin making assumptions and best guesses. This two-dimensional figure appears three-dimensional because the brain interprets it to be that way even though the three-dimensional image does not actually exist.

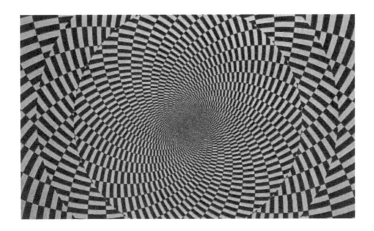

I love the 2012 television commercial with the USS Montana somewhere in the Irish Sea. Seeing a light in the distance, Captain Hancock orders the approaching ship to change its course 15 degrees to the north to avoid a collision.

The reply: "I suggest you change your course 15 degrees to the south to avoid a collision."

Firm and resolute, the Captain replies, "This is the USS Montana, the second largest ship in the North Atlantic fleet. You will change course 15 degrees to the north, or I will be forced to take measures to protect the safety of this ship. Over!"

"This is a lighthouse, mate. It's your call."

The entire bridge crew saw the light off in the distance. They all *knew* it was a ship. They considered no alternatives. How did they get it so wrong? Context. Our brains are constantly making light-speed assumptions and interpretations of the data stimulating our senses, and these assumptions are often based on what it has most frequently encountered in the past.

The crew had only encountered other ships in those waters. They had never seen a lighthouse there. Add in the individual baggage our brains bring to an event (e.g., ego, emotions), and we begin to understand how the bridge crew mistakenly perceived the lighthouse for a ship.

This phenomenon exists across all our senses. Remember *Laurel* versus *Yanny* in 2017? A one-word audio clip became the most divisive subject on the internet since The Dress in 2015. The audio seems to be saying one word – but whether that word is *Yanny* or *Laurel* continues even today to be the source of ardent disagreement. It turns out that about 47% of people hear *Yanny* while 53% of people hear *Laurel*.

Just as our eyes play a role in determining color, our ears play a similar role in our hearing. According to Lars Riecke, a cognitive neuroscientist at Maastricht University in the Netherlands, *Yanny* and *Laurel* sound very similar to our ears regarding timing and energy content although the frequencies are slightly different. Those frequencies that create *Yanny* are higher than those for *Laurel*. If we look at the word in a spectrogram, which graphs the actual sound frequencies that we hear, the word seems to be somewhere between *Yanny* and *Laurel*, so it is an obstruse sound to begin with. When we pay close attention to some frequencies (particularly lower ones), we hear *Laurel*, and when we pay attention to the higher frequencies, we hear *Yanny*. But they are so mixed together and even partially overlapping that our brains have difficulty discerning the truth. Andrew Oxenham, a professor in the Departments of Psychology and Otolaryngology at the University of Minnesota, may have the best (at least honest) answer to this puzzle. "I'm not sure that anyone knows why some people hear it one way and other people hear it another, but that's often the way with these visual and auditory illusions - our brains 'fill in' missing information, and how that happens seems to vary a lot from one person to the next."

One last 'research' example. *Brain Games* is a popular science television series that explores cognitive science by focusing on illusions, psychological experiments, and counterintuitive thinking. One of their episodes speaks directly to how context shapes our perceptions. Brain Games set up a large outdoor stage ostensibly shooting a scene for an upcoming Western movie. Then a car comes out of nowhere striking a parked car on the set. Everyone was in on the fake movie set and car wreck except for the spectators. Each of the spectators was asked several questions. The most important question surrounded the spectator's determination of the speed of the striking vehicle. They asked some of the bystanders, "How fast do you think the vehicle was going when it bumped into the parked car?" About 80 percent of those spectators said 20 mph with a low response of 10 mph. They then asked the same question to other spectators except for a one-word change. "How fast do you think the vehicle was going when it *smashed* into the parked car?" The responses were significantly higher with a high response of 50 mph. Even when confronted with the radar showing the real speed of 20 mph, many of these respondents did not believe it. One word has the power to completely rewrite our perceptions and memories of those perceptions. But it gets better. They then asked, "Did you see the car blow through the stop sign before hitting the parked car?" Typical responses were, "Absolutely!", "Definitely", or "100 percent." Yet, there was no stop sign! These people were being completely honest and struggled to believe the speed of the car and the lack of a stop sign even when confronted with the truth. Even though research suggests our initial perceptions and our memories of those perceptions work in fundamentally different ways (Favila, et al., 2022), both are impacted by context. What we initially perceive and how we remember it over time are always vulnerable to change. In fact, recall of memories becomes less accurate over time not just because of an aging hippocampus but also from a variety of contextual, post-event data. As the narrator of the episode says at the end, "Memories are never a perfect recall of an event."

We Don't Just See the World, We Actively Create It

On a cool Fall evening with my family on the back patio around the firepit sipping our favorite beverages, we watch the boats go by on the Powhatan Creek. We hear the ferry horns blowing as they transport people across the James River. We see bald eagles that bless Jamestown with their presence. We feel the warmth of the fire and smell the smoke billowing from the pit. We feel the breeze Williamsburg enjoys year-round. We engage with one another, even discussing how beautiful the evening is. It appears so clearly to us there is this objective world out there gushing into our minds. Yet, that is just not true. Labels are not attached to the visual signals picked up by our retina or the pressure waves striking our eardrums or the

> *Instead of perception depending largely on signals coming into the brain from the outside world, it depends as much on perceptual predictions flowing in the opposite direction. We don't just passively perceive the world. We actively generate it. The world we experience comes as much, if not more, from the inside out as from the outside in.*
>
> *-- Professor Anil Seth*
> *Neuroscientist*
> *University of Sussex*

molecules stimulating our olfactory neurons. We see the eagles with our eyes, but these are just ambiguous stimuli with no meaning. Our brains must interpret and give meaning to these spurs. And the interpretation is not just identification. Yes, the interpretation of fire means our brain first must identify the fire as fire. But it also brings a wealth of instantaneous additional interpretation. If you are chilled, get closer and the fire will warm you. Or danger…if you touch this fire, you will get burnt. If you directly inhale its smoke for too long, you may die. The perception process may even expose memories of a distant past. We've all experienced a simple smell that instantly transported us back in time to a specific event, a specific time and place.

What we perceive in any given moment is not only informed by what our eyes see, but by a multitude of influences we bring to the table including our physical abilities, cognitive capacities, moods and emotions, stress, social circumstances, values, needs, expectations, cultural influences, and so much more. The interplay of these influences with our senses causes a perpetual feedback loop of learning. Simply, how we interpret our world is not static. Our brain learns from each encounter to better interpret the next time.

How our physical abilities influence our perceptions is fascinating. Research suggests if you are significantly overweight or even tired, distances look further away from you. Renowned Cognitive Psychologist Dennis Proffitt, Professor Emeritus at the University of Virginia, similarly discovered that the capacity to traverse hills affects a person's perception of the slant of that hill. "Our walking ability shapes the apparent walkability of the hill, which determines how we see it. You do not see the hill as it is but rather as it is seen by you." It is not trite to say that increasing our fitness can change the way we see our environment and the people around us. The reality is that it will quite literally transform our perceptions of the world.

Physical abilities are just a part of the grander nature of physicality impacting our perceptions. At 5'7" in height, I imagine my perceptions of the world are very different from someone who is 6'6" - from unconscious perceptions of the cabinet heights in my kitchen (a potential challenge for me) to the height of a typical shower (a potential challenge for him) to the more profound human interactions of leadership, power, and influence. I expect I similarly perceive many aspects of the literal and figurative world differently than my friends of color or friends representing all sorts of diverse backgrounds and experiences.

Consider the adage we all know to be true from our personal experiences - never grocery shop when you are hungry because you will spend a fortune. In other words, whether you are hungry or have a full belly informs your perception of the food in the grocery store at that moment. That perception in turn informs your purchasing behaviors.

I drive a pretty big crew cab truck. My wife loves driving it but hates parking it. She will park as far away from the store as necessary to ease the burden of parking what she refers to as "The Beast." However, I park as close to the building as possible even in the tightest spaces, which utterly mystifies her.

"Jeff, why do you pick the hardest places to park when we could walk another 30 seconds and park away from everyone else?"

"Kat, there is nothing hard about parking where I park."

"This has to go in your next edition of *Perception*. We perceive the difficulty of parking the Beast in very different ways. Backing the truck into tight parking spots is uncomfortable for me but easy for you. Your confidence versus my trepidations with parking the Beast helps our brains interpret the situation. Our perception of parking, particularly regarding ease and difficulty, is very different. And that leads to our choices and subsequently our actions." Boom! Right on Kathy. And that is just scratching the surface of the nuances associated with how we perceive.

Consider the impact of emotions such as fear and uncertainty on our perceptions. Studies consistently have shown that people at the top of a precipice (e.g., hill, balcony) estimate greater distances to the bottom than people at the bottom estimating up. Interestingly, these guesses are often greatly overestimated. One plausible reason is that we fear falling down but do not fear falling up. Father Louis Hennepin was a Belgian Roman Catholic priest of the Franciscan Recollet order and an explorer of the interior of North America. During the winter of 1678-79, he became the first European to document Niagara Falls. Viewing from the top he estimated the height to be 600 feet. He later put to words in *Description de la Louisiane,* a book published in 1683, just how frightening the view was. "The Waters which fall from this horrible Precipice, do foam and boyl after the most hideous manner imaginable, making an outrageous Noise, more terrible than that of Thunder; for when the Wind blows out of the South, their dismal roaring may be heard more than Fifteen Leagues off..." The actual height was just 167 feet. Our perceptions cannot exist without our feelings. As Proffitt and Baer (2020) discovered, "The way you think is endlessly tied to how you feel." And the way we think informs the way we make decisions and ultimately respond to the world and people in our lives.

THE IMPLICATIONS

Things that seem real and universal are just our own individual versions of the world. As distinguished neuroscientist Anil Seth explains, "The truth is that all perceptions are acts of interpretation. They're acts of informed guesswork that the brain applies when it encounters sensory data."

Most people just assume this act of interpretation is consistent with each of us...we all see the world in the same way. Ross and Ward (1996) refer to this lens as naïve realism – the belief that our perceptions are accurate and that everyone else shares these same perceptions. Naïve realism is not so important when talking about which popcorn brand is the best. But it becomes critically important when we discount others' political views, cultural beliefs, religions, beliefs on how to raise our children and what to teach them in school, vaccinations, the role of the police and corrections in our society, and so much more.

Is everyone on my patio perceiving the night in the same way? Of course not. We are seeing very similar things - firepit, beverages, boats, and conversations. Yet, our minds are interpreting these stimuli in different ways. We do share patterns of commonality, which we will discuss as the book progresses, but we also have very distinct ways of interpreting the world around us. Once we accept our perception of the world is subjective and slanted by our biases, we can begin to mitigate our egocentrism. If we begin to understand what factors influence how we perceive our environment, we can perhaps find ways to overcome these influences and make better judgments and decisions. Just the understanding that we see the world differently, sometimes very differently, is incredibly powerful.

Consider *The Dress* or *Laurel* v. *Yanny*. What are the people who hear *Yanny* thinking about the people who hear *Laurel* and vice versa? What is Team Blue and Black thinking about Team White and Gold? I have heard it all in the classroom, but most student responses center around, "They're stupid, biased, ignorant, malicious, or crazy...or a combination." Well, maybe we all have a little of these five characteristics in us, but they have nothing to do with *Laurel* versus *Yanny* or the color of a dress. Psychologists call this form of cognitive bias *Fundamental Attribution Error* - your brain's attempt to explain behavior by placing unwarranted importance on the character and personality of the person rather than contextual, external factors or unconscious, interpretative mechanisms of the body and brain working in tandem. As Dr. Saul McLeod suggests, people tend to assume that people's actions and beliefs depend on what "kind" of person they are rather than a variety of other viable reasons. Go back to how we started this discussion on perception. We believe what we see. We struggle to believe what we do not see. We have difficulty considering the notion that our eyes can betray us and that our interpretations of the world are incorrect. So, it must be something wrong with the other person.

The Blue Dress and *Yanny* versus *Laurel* amplify why it can be so difficult when disagreements arise, and why often good people with good intentions cannot even communicate with one another. Sometimes, we are simply not on the same page from the beginning and are either unable to appreciate we have different lenses or flat-out refuse to acknowledge different people see the world differently. The truth is that our perceptions often are incorrect because each of us makes sense of our world in our own ways. Our perceptions constantly are instilled in our attitudes, words, and actions. However, becoming more open to how and why we see the world as we do is a powerful first step towards mitigating powerful biases and contextual influences impacting our perceptions. We can learn to make more accurately informed decisions and judgments. We can learn to be more open to other people's perspectives. We can improve our communication, empathy, and connectivity across every dimension of our lives.

This is the power of the DISC Behavioral Model. Our DISC profiles, the way we perceive our world and ourselves, are like fingerprints in that they are infinite in number, and no two are exactly the same. Yet, the model does categorize us into groups and subgroups who tend to look at the world more similarly. The DISC model recognizes our similarities but also brings to life the unique lens through which each of us perceives the entirety of our world. Most importantly, it gives us the tools to change our perceptions, which in turn will change our behaviors.

DISC ORIGINS

2

Historical Foundations of the DISC Model

Written aptitude tests have been around for centuries. However, the first true psychometric testing was conducted by Francis Galton in the 1880s demonstrating that objective tests could provide meaningful scores. Galton was one of the first experimental psychologists and the founder of Differential Psychology,

the study of psychological differences between people rather than their shared characteristics. He virtually started from nothing having to create the requisite tools including statistical methods, correlation and regression, which are now staples of the human sciences.

Although assessments are a fairly recent endeavor, efforts have been made to understand human development and behavior from the earliest of recorded history. The desire to find ways of describing what people do, how they do it, and even why they do it is not new. The Greeks are credited with developing the first organized method of describing personality types. They believed that the four basic human liquids – blood, phlegm, yellow bile, and black bile – were responsible for different kinds of personality. Hippocrates created a personality development theory surrounding these basic liquids, which was used until the Middle Ages. Other systems of thought, like numerology and astrology, attempted to clarify the mysteries of human behavior and still have their followers today. Chinese philosophical approaches to personality originated as far back as the 8th to 6th century BC. *Shangshu*, a renowned writing of that period, offered a personality taxonomy that had significant influence on subsequent Chinese personality theories.

Fast forwarding to the late 1800s, Sigmund Freud began the psychological school of thought concerning human behavior. Key to his psychoanalytic theory is the view that personality is fashioned progressively as the individual passes through various psychosexual stages. He defined the human organism as a dynamic, complex system composed of physical and psychic energy. Both supporters and critics of his theory of personality development regard it as a significant contribution in the study of human development.

During the latter years of the 19th century, sociology and anthropology began to emerge as independent disciplines. According to these new social sciences, people are products of the society in which they live. One's behavior is shaped more by social circumstances than by biological factors. Alfred Adler, Karen Horney, Erich Fromm, and Harry Sullivan were early pioneers in the study of the social nature of human development. Consistent with all four theorists is the notion that personality is interpersonal. Personality is a relationship between and among people.

Based upon Freudian theory, Erikson created a conceptual structure for the complete life cycle. Erickson primarily was interested in psychosocial development. He was concerned with the development of the person within a social context. Erickson asserted that human development follows the epigenetic principle. This term suggests that each stage builds upon, and in relation to, preceding ones. Each part of the personality has a particular time in the life span when it must evolve if it is going to at all. Should a stage not mature on schedule, the rest of the individual's personality growth is unfavorably altered.

Theorists, such as Ivan Pavlov, John Watson, and B.F. Skinner, suggested a behavioral approach to the study of human development. Behaviorists are interested in how people learn to behave in particular ways. Rejecting an innate theory of behavioral evolution, they believed that human nature can be fully understood by studying environmental stimuli. Consider the *Pavlovian Experiment*. While researching digestion responses in dogs, Pavlov determined that he could predict that dogs would salivate when food was placed in their mouth. He soon discovered that this response occurred even before the food was provided. Because the sound of the door had consistently come before the presentation of the food to the mouth, the dogs had conveyed the salivary response to these actions. In the view of behaviorists, individuals are simply mediators between environmental stimulus and human response.

In the early 1900s, Carl Gustav Jung, known as the father of analytical psychology, asserted that personality could be oriented in one of two directions: extroversion or introversion. Jung attributed the difference in personality styles to the way we think and process information. He described four components of personality: Sensing, intuition, feeling, and thinking. Jung intended to explain the forces affecting human behavior and to identify core personality traits that differ among people. Jung was acutely aware of the role of our environment regarding our response to the world. He believed humans are born with many predispositions. Our behavior generally will be determined by the effect of human experience with these characteristics. In other words, an individual's responses to the world are the results of inner forces acting upon and being acted upon by external forces.

In the 1920s, Dr. William Marston expanded Jung's personality theory by describing human emotional responses to one's surroundings. A Harvard University educated psychologist and lawyer, Marston was a keen intellect with a variety of interests and contributions to society. One of the themes of his life surrounded the championing of women. He was a fervent supporter of women's rights including the use of birth control and the right to vote. Interestingly, Marston was the creator of the Wonder Woman character as he saw educational value in comics and another path of advocacy for women through the character. Marston was also fascinated by deception. While working on his undergraduate degree at Harvard, he conducted studies in 1913 trying to measure the bodily symptoms of deception at the Harvard Psychological Lab. In the 1920s, Marston and his wife developed an early lie detector machine (a systolic blood-pressure test), which later evolved into the modern-day polygraph.

Marston's greatest contribution to psychology rested in his explanation of human behavior. He theorized each of us behaves according to how we view our surroundings and how we view ourselves in relation to those surroundings. Thus, one of the most significant themes of this text emerges – Perception drives behavior. Marston presented his research findings in his 1928 book, *Emotions of Normal People.* He published a second book in 1931 titled *Integrative Psychology.*

Marston's book or model did not achieve notoriety at the time, and Marston never created a behavioral assessment based on his model. The history of the DISC assessment began in the 1940s with psychologist Walter Clarke. Clarke built a test for employ selection called the Activity Vector Analysis. After gathering and analyzing the data on this instrument, he discovered the four factors produced from his data sounded a lot like Marston's DISC model. The first DISC assessment of sorts, "*Self* Discription", was developed by Clarke's company providing empirical support for Marston's model.

Marston's work paved the way for the multitude and variety of DISC Assessments we have today as well as an entire global industry surrounding the model. According to a recent New York Times article, psychometric testing is a $500 million industry with well over 2,500 instruments on the market. The two most prevalent assessments are DISC and MBTI (*Meyers Brigg*) accounting alone for millions of assessments each year. The Center for Police Leadership & Ethics recently released the powerfully valuable and accurate *DISC 17 Self-Assessment* included in this book.

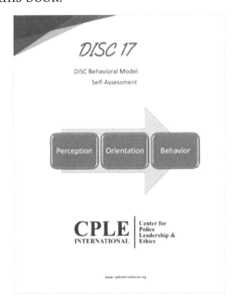

Benefits (and Dangers) of the DISC Model

3

DISC begins with self-awareness, but it does not stop there. It also develops "other awareness" and "situation awareness." DISC is about discovering the patterns of observable behavioral styles of self, others, and the response to the changing demands of the environment. People are different, yet they are predictably different. Predicting our responses to the environment leads to the many values of the model.

DISC is a tremendous tool to assist each of us in a variety of areas: awareness, preventing burnout, understanding individual motives, increasing tolerance, reducing unhealthy conflict, and improving our communications with others. We begin the chapter with the benefits and

> *If you know others*
> *and know yourself,*
> *you need not fear the*
> *result of a hundred battles;*
> *If you know yourself but not*
> *others, for every victory, you*
> *will also suffer a defeat;*
> *If you know neither yourself*
> *nor others, you will*
> *succumb in every battle.*
> —Sun Tzu

value of the model; we end it discussing dangers and misuses of the model if used for purposes beyond its scope and reach.

Know Thyself and Know Others

Sun Tzu's famous remarks are clearly about winning in battle. However, his insights may be applied to winning in any area, any battle, or any challenge. Sun Tzu's remarks highlight the need not only to know oneself, but also to know others. Goleman (1997, p.47) described an old Japanese tale in which a belligerent samurai challenged an old Zen master to explain the concept of heaven and hell.

The monk replied with scorn, "You're nothing but a lout—I can't waste my time with the likes of you!"

His honor attacked, the samurai flew into a rage and pulled his sword from its scabbard. He yelled at the monk, "I could kill you for your impertinence."

"That," the monk replied, "is hell."

Recognizing the truth in the master's point about the fury and rage that had gripped him, the samurai calmed down and sheathed his sword, then he bowed and thanked the monk for the insight.

"And that," said the monk, "is heaven."

The samurai's sudden understanding of his own agitated state illustrated the crucial difference between being caught up in a feeling and becoming aware of being swept away by it. True self-awareness involves looking squarely in the mirror and recognizing not only our strengths but also our areas for growth, quite often known to us as our blind spots. Each of us has blind spots. In fact, blind spots are often strengths which are being underused or overused.

Any misused strength may instantly become a very strong liability. For instance, the soft-spoken, humble nature of a leader may endear him to us, but being too soft-spoken and humble may give the appearance of a lack of confidence, competence, and strength. DISC would have us play to our strengths as well as address our weaknesses, particularly in the context of human relations.

The DISC model also offers affirmation. Because we respond to our environment differently than someone else does not make us crazy or broken. We all are different, and that is as it should be. I received an email from a former student a couple of years ago. I get a lot of emails, texts, and calls from students. Most are surface level, just "thanks for a great class." Some push back on me concerning a concept or something I said in class. From time to time, a few go deeper, like this one.

> Hi Jeff
>
> I assume you've had a lot thank you emails this weekend after last week's class. I apologize for not sending my appreciation sooner. To be honest, sending a thank you email to an instructor is not something I do, like never. But your class was different.
>
> Prior to attending the class, I was ready to hang up my hat at work. I love my job. I love that my profession allows me to help people every day. But I'm not very liked by my supervisors. It's partly because I'm the only woman in my small organization although I know it's more than that as well. I had just had it with constantly getting beat down and not being able to please everyone. Weak, I know, but…well, that's who I am. Coming to this class was going to be my last hoorah in my organization.
>
> Your class showed me I don't have to be someone else like I have been told time and again by my supervisors. I don't know if you noticed last week, but I like to smile. Apparently, my bosses read my smile and friendliness as being soft or weak. My dad used to call me happy go lucky when I was little. I wasn't sure that was a good thing until now. The DISC class showed that it takes all kinds of people to make the world work. No one personality is better than the other. We all can be failures, and yes, we all can be successes! Most of all what I learned is that people follow people more than they do rank, position, or anything else. I like that. I'd rather be a good person who cares about people than to be liked by my supervisors.
>
> Once again, thank you. It was a wonderful class!

Her email sparked several conversations over the following few weeks—conversations in which, I think she would agree, we both grew. Emails like this inspire me. DISC has the capacity to profoundly impact so many people in so many meaningful ways. Over two thousand years ago, Socrates asserted that knowledge of self is the most important of all wisdom. Self-examination, he taught, led not only to insight in directing ourselves, but permitted us to understand the motives of others. The DISC model offers a method for individuals to better understand and appreciate themselves and their behavior and to improve their flexibility and effectiveness in a variety of situations.

Understanding Individual Motives

People differ not only in their skills and abilities, but also in their motives, commitment, and confidence. Motives may be described as needs, wants, or drives—those powers that influence individuals to move in a specific direction. While individuals may have hundreds of competing needs or wants at any given time, behavior usually is affected by the strongest need at that specific moment (Hersey, 2001).

Some motives appear to be universal. Most individuals want to feel involved in the decisions that affect them. They want to be recognized for a job well done. They want to be valued as an individual with specific talents and contributions. Covey (1989) suggested, "Next to physical survival, the greatest need of a human being is psychological survival—to be understood, to be affirmed, to be validated, to be appreciated."

Other motives appear to be more individually appropriate. No one person has the same blends of needs as another, and we must understand which motives are most important to us as individuals. The DISC model can be an effective tool to this end. The different behavioral dimensions have different mixtures and intensities of motives. DISC assists us in what many of us already do—taking conscious effort to empathize with people and trying to view situations through their lens.

Confucius offered, "Look at the means which a man employs, consider his motives, observe his pleasures. A man simply cannot conceal himself!" Identifying other's DISC profile and understanding their wants and needs can be of significant assistance to each of us attempting to inspire ourselves and others.

Preventing Burnout

Burnout occurs when people feel overwhelmed, undervalued, or when they perceive nothing of value coming from their efforts. Burnout increases when leaders and peers are unwilling to demonstrate the value of their workforce and fully engage with one another. Frustration and a sense of under-appreciation may consume them.

Anyone in *any* endeavor can experience burnout. It can happen at work, home, church, school, our associations, and teams. Burnout may present itself in the form of anger, bitterness, discouragement, weariness, struggles going to work, or lack of attentiveness. Burnout, left unchecked, also may lead to more serious emotional and physical illnesses as well as harming relationships with those around us.

No two people will behave or react in the same way to their environment because they have different personalities and learned experiences leading to different perceptions. Burnout prevention is an individual process. Maybe the most important technique we can exercise to prevent burnout is to get to know ourselves and others better. When we understand our natural anxieties and responses, as well as those of others, we can take a more productive, proactive approach to effectively deal with stressful situations.

INCREASED TOLERANCE

Buber (1963) observed, "In a genuine dialogue each of the partners, even when he stands in opposition to the other, heeds, affirms, and confirms his opponent as an existing other." Prejudices are a kind of emotional learning that occurs early in life, making these responses especially hard to eradicate entirely, even in people who as adults feel it is wrong to hold them. Prejudices are formed in childhood, while the beliefs that are used to justify them come later. Later in life people may want to change their prejudices, but it is far easier to change intellectual beliefs than deep feelings. It may be human nature to be more accepting of people with similar appearances, cultural backgrounds, values, and experiences. Yet, successful people are tolerant to the needs, preferences, and differences of others.

The DISC model offers a measure of explanation for people's behavior. It can help individuals understand that what may seem bizarre behavior to them is very natural for someone else. We are not *all* crazy (well, we're no crazier than the next person). The DISC model provides the rationale that everyone is different, and that difference is normal. Each of us can try to develop a more tolerant outlook by learning about the differences in people and developing confidence and an open mind in ourselves. Even though some conflict (and confrontation) is inherent in human nature and even productive, cohesion and mutual tolerance are absolute requirements of social functioning (Gardner, 1990).

REDUCING UNHEALTHY CONFLICT

Conflict is an unequivocal characteristic of any endeavor involving human beings. From gossip and rumors to substantive and emotional disagreements to matters of character and values, conflict is part of who we are. Conflict sometimes manifests as brief, explosive outbursts, and other times hides silently but powerfully beneath the surface. When conflict is managed negatively, it can have destructive and polarizing consequences. However, when managed positively, it can provide constructive and mutually satisfying results.

Marston developed the DISC model on the premise that different people behave differently in different situations. However, most people tend to behave in one or two primary dimensions most of the time. Similarly, most individuals have one or two preferred styles for managing conflict. Identifying those preferred styles with a goal toward developing other strategies for resolution might help ensure constructive outcomes.

The desire and ability to understand and communicate effectively are the most important abilities we have in formulating strategies for effectively managing conflict. Even considering external factors and influences, each of us has the power to oversee our emotions and behaviors. I even believe we have a good chance in times of conflict to somewhat control the behaviors of others.

Dr. Wayne Dyer offered, "I cannot always control what goes on outside. But I can always control what goes on inside." I would take Dr. Dyer's assertion a step further. By controlling what goes on inside, we begin to control what goes on outside. DISC is distinctively capable of assisting each of us to develop and improve these necessary skills.

IMPROVING COMMUNICATIONS

> *What is peculiarly characteristic of the human world is above all else, something takes place between one being and another the like of which can be found nowhere in nature.*
> —Martin Buber

Effective communication provides the foundation for all successful relationships. When the individuals involved understand each other, the potential for effective communication is dramatically increased. When people can recognize the behavioral style of others, they are better equipped to effectively relate to that person's unique style. Sometimes, we must interact with other people by setting limits, confronting them, or engaging them in exciting activities. At other times, we may need to take a quiet approach and let the person solve problems on their own.

It is easy to communicate from our own perch, our own comfort zone. When I engage an employee in a tough conversation about not meeting my expectations, I like to be direct and clear. I don't like the sandwich approach where the boss says something nice, then offers the the negative, and concludes with something nice—there's just too much opportunity in that mess for the message and intent to be lost. My comfort zone may be completely appropriate when talking with an employee who shares my behavioral preferences. However, what about the employee who is very sensitive to criticism, or the employee who needs a longer conversation in the narrative as opposed to the bullet points I might prefer?

The best leaders consider the needs and behavioral

preferences of others when they communicate, not their own needs. DISC is uniquely positioned to assist us in this uncomfortable arena. In chapter 8, we will explore improving communications with those who have different personalities and behavioral preferences.

Misuses of DISC

The DISC model is profound, scientifically based, and of tremendous value across countless contexts in our lives. Yet, it can be completely misused, leading to frustration and potential complications, which we'll discuss here.

Labeling

Labeling people is fraught with potential problems. We all know the dangers associated with stereotypes, stigma, and bias. One of the main pitfalls associated with labeling people regarding their personality is what I refer to as the self-licking lollipop. When we label someone, even if the label is predominantly correct, that person may so embrace that label, that role, that he is held captive by it even in situations in he would otherwise act differently. For instance, if we label a person as dominant and powerful, that person may start to act that way even in times where he would normally act in a different way. The labeling, in effect, becomes a self-fulfilling prophesy.

Misuse also may be subtle at times, such as assuming a person with control issues cannot be supportive or follow others. Or perhaps we assume a person who likes to be the center of attention cannot be quiet and let others take center stage. We should never limit anyone's growth by holding them prisoner to their natural preferences. Each of us can act in any way we choose throughout the day.

The dangers of labeling also increase when we continue to broaden the labels. For instance, it may be intuitive to refer to the confident, powerful personality as a lion or leader of the pack. However, when we do that, we infer confident, powerful personalities automatically make good leaders, which is not always the case. We also infer other personalities are not capable of being the boss or leader of the pack. We know this is not the case.

Be careful of the self-fulfilling prophecy and stigma traps sometimes associated with labeling. If we are not mindful, we can turn an incredibly valuable instrument designed to build and maintain relationships into something that damages and alienates those around us.

Using the Model to Excuse or Justify Behavior

Another misuse of the model occurs when we look the other way or shrug off someone's bad or inappropriate behavior, justifying their actions as "that's just how they are wired." Even worse is when we justify our own actions.

A parent lets her son get away with overly rebellious behavior because that's just how he is. The boss tends to look the other way when one of his employees frequently runs late because that's just the way that employee is. Maybe a co-worker is not held accountable for accuracy in her reports and products because she is more of a big-picture person. Or perhaps we expect more from another employee because he always produces a perfect product. Obviously, all of these reactions may be unfair to the employees as well as those around them.

The potential for misuse intensifies the more we know about the DISC model—the more we begin to categorize certain behaviors with certain profiles. Understanding your DISC profile can help explain, even justify, your decisions, but it is not meant to become a roadmap etched in stone. Our natural preferences should never become excuses to limit or justify our decisions and expectations of others.

The DISC model assists in identifying people's natural responses to the world. It should never be used as an excuse to hold people more accountable than others or to excuse or justify people's bad behavior.

Using the Assessment as a Mental Health or Emotional Assessment

Two years ago I was teaching a week-long leadership class in the Midwest. As the first morning progressed, I took time to provide a little explanation of how the week would look. I explained a full day would be committed to the DISC behavioral model and assessment later in the week. A student raised his hand.

"Jeff, no disrespect to you or the curriculum, but I've taken the DISC assessment five times in the past four years at work. I just can't handle another instructor telling me how f*d up I am one more time."

This was not the first time I had encountered this comment. In fact, I gave up counting over the years.

Most of the time, the culprit for this blatantly incorrect use of the model is an inexperienced facilitator. No nationally required certifications exist to teach the model or give the assessment. This lack of consistency and accreditation of instructor and curriculum competencies may lead to misunderstandings, some of which have very detrimental results. Sometimes the culprit is a single manager in the company or even an organizational culture out to place value labels on its employees.

Regardless of the reason, the DISC model was not designed to address pathology or mental health. Much of the research in human behavior in the early 20th century did focus on mental health, but the DISC model resulted from Marston's curiosity in the behavior of typical people. Just the name of his renowned book describing the model should be a clue—*The Emotions of Normal People*. While we all get a little frustrated from time to time with people who have different personalities and behavioral preferences, one is no better or worse than the other. And certainly, none indicate mental or emotional deficiencies.

EMPLOYMENT PROFILING

Many companies and recruiters use the DISC model to hire and promote employees. For instance, a sales recruiter may look exclusively for an applicant with an outgoing personality coupled with high energy and enthusiasm. While this type of person may be great at sales, he also may not be. Conversely, it would be a travesty to assume a person with a different personality, perhaps more task-oriented and reserved, would not be great in sales.

An accounting firm may be more interested in hiring a detail-oriented CPA who is comfortable spending her days buried in tax records. Yet, I personally know very outgoing, people-oriented accountants who are fantastic at their job.

Consider the following assertions found on the Internet, advertising the benefits of the DISC assessment:

> *DISC profiling enables companies to find out about the various personality traits of an individual. It can help determine the ways in which people will react to new challenges, or how they are likely to behave in a team*

environment. It can help your company hire and pro-mote for success.

By understanding the predictable behaviors, communi-cation styles, strengths within a team, and preferences in the workplace, one can hire the right person for the work environment, which will help them to succeed. By under-standing their sales style, you'll know whether they are a match for the type of sales you are doing, and whether they are compatible with this type of selling.

These are very dangerous assertions.

DISC can be of tremendous value to individuals and or-ganizations. The model offers self-awareness, other-awareness, better communications, and increased tolerance. It can even be used successfully as a tool to frame conversations during hiring and promotion interviews. However, it is fraught with danger when specifically used to choose whom to hire or promote. In fact, this use may be illegal, depending on the specific applica-tion and the laws in your state.

The DISC model measures how we typically view and respond to the world. It does *not* measure the entirety of a person. It does not measure personality; rather, it assesses the observable behavior people display. It does not measure skills, work ethic, judgment, maturity, aptitude, or even character. DISC does not measure or accurately predict success in any endeavor.

Companies all over the world use DISC for human resources reasons, unfortunately. Consider evading this trap. All four profile dimensions have strengths and weaknesses. All four can be good or bad at anything in life. The maturity and wisdom to choose which dimension to display in the appropriate circumstance is the real value of the model.

PITTING ONE PROFILE OVER ANOTHER

No behavioral profile is better than another. Judging others based on their profile or attempting to change them to a behavioral profile that we prefer is an incorrect misuse of the model. All profiles have strengths and weaknesses, mostly surrounding the appropriate time and circumstances to employ different behaviors. DISC is value-free. DISC does not predict success.

You cannot pass or fail the DISC assessment, and there is no such thing as a better or worse profile.

For several years, I conducted research at the FBI Academy on this very premise, focusing on the relationship between behavioral preferences and leadership. My research was driven by one simple, overarching question:

To what extent do behavioral profiles predict leadership effectiveness?

To be technical for a moment: Regression analysis was conducted to determine potential relationships between the predictor variable of behavioral profile and the criterion variable of leadership effectiveness, albeit I had already used chi-square analysis establishing no significant associations. No significant findings ($p < .05$) were found using an analysis of variance. No predictive value or significant relationships existed between behavioral profiles and leadership effectiveness.

More simply: People of *all* DISC profiles can become exceptional leaders.

CLOSING THOUGHTS

One of the qualities that distinguishes humans from other animals is our intense desire to understand ourselves and others. Throughout history, people have tried not only to describe human behavior, but also to answer the question of why people behave the way they do. A *why* question, however, demands a causal explanation—a linear *because* response.

A more useful endeavor may be to question *how* or in what way something happens (Anderson, 1999). The DISC model was created by Dr. William Marston to offer insights into *how* humans behave.

DISC measures innate traits and learned behavior to build a more complete picture of one's style or approach to a given situation. It is a system for understanding how people behave. DISC assists in describing how people deal with power, motivation, change, rules and policies, and even each other. DISC is not value-based; there is no single best behavioral style.

DISC helps us understand and appreciate our natural differences. It is all too easy to pass judgement on others and assume they are irrational or are overtly trying to annoy us. Carl Jung, a key figure in the development of the psychological underpinnings of the DISC model, offered, "If one does not understand a person, one tends to regard him as a fool."

The truth is, most people are not fools. They are just different from one another in the way they process and respond to the world. Once we really accept this notion, we increase our tolerance and lessen our conflict. We begin to see what motivates different people, what fears we share and do not share, and how some of us hate conflict when others thrive in it. DISC provides a language and process for better communications and more constructive conflict as opposed to destructive confrontation. The more we understand our natural behavioral predispositions, the better we can influence both ourselves and others.

We are not animals. We are not a product of what has happened to us in our past. We have the power of choice.
—Steven Covey

The DISC model has numerous practical implications for any type of endeavor associated with human connectivity. DISC provides a method for increased self-awareness, understanding, tolerance, and appreciation of people with different styles of behaving. DISC can provide crucial assistance in team building and conflict resolution whether at work, home or play.

Perhaps most importantly, DISC provides the basis for flexibility and adaptability. It provides the necessary information to adjust our behavior to the fluid requirements and needs of the situation and the people around us. The model can be misused and misapplied, but used in the appropriate manner, the benefits of the model are profound.

Let's get started!

DISC-17©

THE ASSESSMENT

4

ABOUT OUR DISC BEHAVIORAL ASSESSMENT (DISC-17)

The DISC-17 assessment comprises 24 groups of descriptors; the groups are arranged in a forced-choice format with four words in each group. You must choose the two words that *most* and *least* describe you from the four choices in each of the 24 groupings. You may find none of the words in a group seems correct, or perhaps multiple words accurately characterize you.

To the best of your ability, choose the most and least accurate words. The model recognizes the *most* descriptor may not always describe you perfectly, and similarly, the *least* descriptor does not mean you never display that characteristic.

For this book, I'm using the ipsative or forced-choice format because I believe it's the best method to gain accurate data and results in assessments such as this. It is simple, consistent, and more easily compared to other participants' assessments. It eliminates the *don't know, neutral,* and *not applicable* responses found in many other surveys. Participants must commit to an answer. Perhaps the most important benefit of this formatting is the mitigation of bias such as social desirability or response bias.

A FEW THOUGHTS BEFORE YOU BEGIN

The DISC-17 assessment is not a test. There are no right or wrong responses, just as there are no right or wrong results. Be honest with yourself when choosing your responses. It is very easy to answer the responses from the mindset of *Who I Want to Be.* For the results to be accurate, push through that natural desire and respond from a view of *Who I Really Am.*

I suggest initially attempting the assessment with a broad lens—just your preferences in general. However, adding a contextual framework may help you decide between two responses if you find yourself having difficulty narrowing the choices from four to one. You may need to put yourself in a specific context when responding, such as home, work, church, sports, etc.

The instrument, however, is designed to accommodate this very issue. The first time I took the assessment, I commented to my colleague, "There were several questions that could have gone either way between two words." He said, "Ok, take it again and answer those questions with the other word." Both times I had the same specific pattern.

Context plays one more significant role. Words mean different things in different settings. Consider the word *talkative*. An extrovert who is all about people and engagement obviously would identify with this word. Yet, a person who detests large crowds and public speaking also may identify with this word if they are talkative in their small work groups or with family. Again, placing yourself in a specific context at least will offer consistency in your focus.

Many of you feel conflicted while taking the assessment and are sure you're contradicting yourself. Don't let that bother you. Most of us feel that way, and 99% of the time it does not affect the outcomes of the assessment. One percent of assessments has responses that contradict other responses so much that they cancel each other out. We will talk about that later; do not fret over the extremely low possibility. Just be honest with yourself on each of the 24 questions.

Finally, don't spend too much time on each question. Give each question its due diligence, but research over the years generally shows results are more accurate when respondents go with their first choice as opposed to overanalyzing the options.

LET'S GET STARTED

DISC-17 comprises 24 groups of descriptors. The groups are arranged in a forced-choice format with four words in each group.

Place **one** check mark or X in the **Most** column to describe which word best describes you. Place **one** check mark or X in the **Least** column to describe which word least describes you.

Example

	MOST	LEAST
Eager	X	
Brave		
Rule-oriented		
Tactful		X

Response Page 1

Choose one Most and one Least in each of the 24 groups of words

		M	L				M	L
1.	Eager			5.	Steady		
	Brave				Bold		
	Rules - oriented				Spontaneous		
	Tactful				Exact		
2.	Careful			6.	Aggressive		
	Candid				Convincing		
	Persuasive				Kind		
	Sincere				Specific		
3.	Life of the Party			7.	Enthusiastic		
	Precise				Methodical		
	Opinionated				Assertive		
	Calm				Good- natured		
4.	Inspiring			8.	Caring		
	Decisive				Logical		
	Conforming				Exciting		
	Detailed				Daring		

Response Page 2

Choose one Most and one Least in each of the 24 groups of words

		M	L
9.	Captivating		
	Cooperative		
	Determined		
	Compliant		
10.	Obliging		
	Stimulating		
	Guarded		
	Outspoken		
11.	Iron-willed		
	Structured		
	Animated		
	Neighborly		
12.	Eloquent		
	Perfectionist		
	Courageous		
	Passive		

		M	L
13.	Systematic		
	Charismatic		
	Domineering		
	Sympathetic		
14.	Extrovert		
	Direct		
	Inflexible		
	Content		
15.	Popular		
	Submissive		
	Fearless		
	Disciplined		
16.	Neutral		
	Impulsive		
	Predictable		
	Powerful		

Response Page 3

Choose one Most and one Least in each of the 24 groups of words

	M	L
17. Sensitive		
Vibrant		
Orderly		
Impatient		
18. Controlling		
Withdrawn		
Sincere		
Unplanned		
19. Easygoing		
Outgoing		
Stubborn		
Forceful		
20. Fun-loving		
Loyal		
Imposing		
Organized		

	M	L
21. Jovial		
Detailed		
Audacious		
Soft-spoken		
22. Cheerful		
Risk-taker		
Talkative		
Prepared		
23. Center of Attention		
Passive		
Thorough		
Overbearing		
24. Factual		
Helpful		
Magnetic		
Urgent		

RESPONSE ANALYSIS INSTRUCTIONS

1. On the following pages, circle the letter under the **Most** column and the **Least** column in each grouping that corresponds to your responses on the assessment.

Example

	Response			**Response Analysis Page**	
	MOST	LEAST		MOST	LEAST
Eager	X			(I)	I
Brave				D	D
Rule-oriented				S	S
Tactful		X		C	(C)

Response Analysis Page 1

		M	L
1.	Eager	I	I
	Brave	D	D
	Rules - oriented	C	C
	Tactful	S	S

		M	L
5.	Steady	S	S
	Bold	D	D
	Spontaneous	I	I
	Exact	C	C

		M	L
2.	Careful	C	C
	Candid	D	D
	Persuasive	I	I
	Sincere	S	S

		M	L
6.	Aggressive	D	D
	Convincing	I	I
	Kind	S	S
	Specific	C	C

		M	L
3.	Life of the Party	I	I
	Precise	C	C
	Opinionated	D	D
	Calm	S	S

		M	L
7.	Enthusiastic	I	I
	Methodical	C	C
	Assertive	D	D
	Good-natured	S	S

		M	L
4.	Inspiring	I	I
	Decisive	D	D
	Conforming	S	S
	Detailed	C	C

		M	L
8.	Caring	S	S
	Logical	C	C
	Exciting	I	I
	Daring	D	D

Response Analysis Page 2

		M	L				M	L
9.	Captivating	I	I	13.	Systematic	C	C
	Cooperative	S	S		Charismatic	I	I
	Determined	D	D		Domineering	D	D
	Compliant	C	C		Sympathetic	S	S
10.	Obliging	S	S	14.	Extrovert	I	I
	Stimulating	I	I		Direct	D	D
	Guarded	C	C		Inflexible	C	C
	Outspoken	D	D		Content	S	S
11.	Iron-willed	D	D	15.	Popular	I	I
	Structured	C	C		Submissive	S	S
	Animated	I	I		Fearless	D	D
	Neighborly	S	S		Disciplined	C	C
12.	Eloquent	I	I	16.	Neutral	S	S
	Perfectionist	C	C		Impulsive	I	I
	Courageous	D	D		Predictable	C	C
	Passive	S	S		Powerful	D	D

Response Analysis Page 3

	M	L
17. Sensitive	S	S
Vibrant	I	I
Orderly	C	C
Impatient	D	D
18. Controlling	D	D
Withdrawn	C	C
Sincere	S	S
Unplanned	I	I
19. Easygoing	S	S
Outgoing	I	I
Stubborn	C	C
Forceful	D	D
20. Fun-loving	I	I
Loyal	S	S
Imposing	D	D
Organized	C	C

	M	L
21. Jovial	I	I
Detailed	C	C
Audacious	D	D
Soft-spoken	S	S
22. Cheerful	S	S
Risk-taker	D	D
Talkative	I	I
Prepared	C	C
23. Center of Attention	I	I
Passive	S	S
Thorough	C	C
Overbearing	D	D
24. Factual	C	C
Helpful	S	S
Magnetic	I	I
Urgent	D	D

RESPONSE ANALYSIS INSTRUCTIONS CONTINUED...

2. Record the following numbers under **Your Numbers**. Count all the **Ds** you circled in the **Most** columns in all 24 responses. Write that number in the Most column on the **D** row. Count all the **Is** you circled in the Most columns in all 24 responses. Write that number in the Most column on the **I** row. Continue this with the **Ss** and **Cs**. When the Most column is complete, continue the same process with the Least column.

3. Using the **D** row, subtract the **Least** column number from the **Most** column number and write that number in the **Results** row (Most—Least = Results). Then repeat this process for the I, S, and C rows. *Note: You will have negative numbers in your results.*

Sample

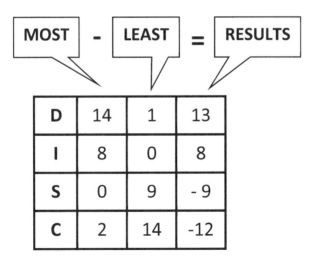

MOST	-	LEAST	=	RESULTS

	MOST	LEAST	RESULTS
D	14	1	13
I	8	0	8
S	0	9	- 9
C	2	14	-12

Your Numbers

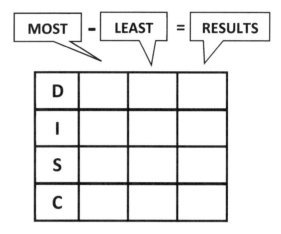

4. Using the numbers from the **Results** column, circle the corresponding numbers for D, I, S, and C on **Your Graph**.

5. Connect the circles on the graph from left to right with straight lines.

• Please see the sample graph based on the preceding numbers. You will notice in the participant's highest dimension is D with the second highest dimension being I. We would categorize this person's DISC profile as a D/I. The nuances in the high and lows of these two dimensions above the bold horizontal line, as well as the two below the line, matter. But the D/I designation is a good place to start in identifying this participant's natural perceptions and responses to the world.

Sample

D	I	S	C
19	19	19	19
17	17	17	17
15	15	15	15
13	13	13	13
11	11	11	11
9	9	9	9
7	7	7	7
5	5	5	5
3	3	3	3
1	1	1	1
-1	-1	-1	-1
-3	-3	-3	-3
-5	-5	-5	-5
-7	-7	-7	-7
-9	-9	-9	-9
-11	-11	-11	-11
-13	-13	-13	-13
-15	-15	-15	-15
-17	-17	-17	-17
-19	-19	-19	-19

YOUR GRAPH

D	I	S	C
19	19	19	19
17	17	17	17
15	15	15	15
13	13	13	13
11	11	11	11
9	9	9	9
7	7	7	7
5	5	5	5
3	3	3	3
1	1	1	1
-1	-1	-1	-1
-3	-3	-3	-3
-5	-5	-5	-5
-7	-7	-7	-7
-9	-9	-9	-9
-11	-11	-11	-11
-13	-13	-13	-13
-15	-15	-15	-15
-17	-17	-17	-17
-19	-19	-19	-19

6. Find a reasonable facsimile of your graph on the following pages and circle the Quadrant number found in the angle of the Quadrant. If one of your dimensions is right on the line, consider it to be below the line for the purpose of finding a match. As there are infinite numbers of specific profiles, and DISC is just as much about your dimensions below the line as it is your dimensions above the line, it is not practical or necessary to be exact.

A small percentage of people have profiles with a single dimension above the line and three below (about 5%). We depicted those graphs using Quadrants 1 through 4. Most of us (about 80%) have two DISC dimensions above the line and two below the line, which are depicted with Quadrants 5 through 12. Roughly 15% of profiles have three dimensions above the line and one below. The DISC-17 instrument also uses Quadrants 5 through 12 to handle these profiles without calling them out specifically.

Within the group with two above and two below, two combinations are so rare that many instruments pay little to no attention to them—the I and C combination (I/C or C/I) and the D and S combination (D/S or S/D). Because they are just as significant as the other more common or classic profiles, DISC-17 gives them their own unique narratives. These profiles are represented by quadrants 13 through 16. The final profile depicted in this text is shown in Quadrant 17—the tight or compressed pattern.

1/3 DISC Dimensions

Use this page if your graph has **one dimension above** the bold horizontal line and **three** below the line. Look in the quadrant that matches your top-ranking dimension.

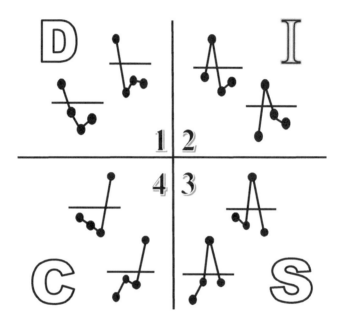

Using the number located in the Quadrant angle (1-4), find the corresponding page with your narrative description. Read the narrative and see how accurately it describes you.

Common 2/2 DISC Dimensions

Find your equivalent draft on this page if you have two dimensions above the line in the more usual combinations: D/I, I/S, S/C, and C/D, (or the reverse, of course: I/D, D/C, C/S, and S/I). These are clockwise or counter-clockwise graphs that cross the center line once.

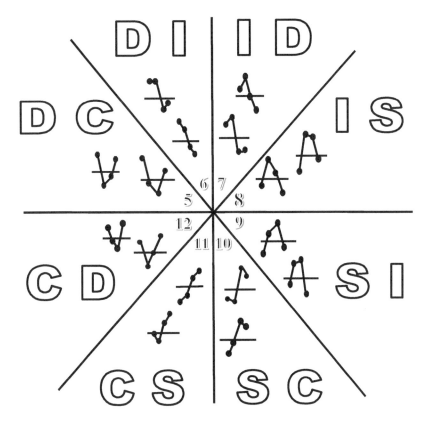

Using the number located in the Quadrant angle (5-12), find the corresponding page with your narrative description. Read the narrative and see how accurately it describes you.

However, if your top two dimensions are S/D or I/C (or the reverse), move to the next page.

A FEW UNCOMMON BUT JUST AS IMPORTANT GRAPHS
DIAGONAL COMBINATIONS

Most two-dimension combinations follow the axis in a clockwise or counter clockwise manner. For example, common two-dimension combinations are D/I, I/S, S/C, and C/D (or the reverse: I/D, D/C, C/S, and S/I). However, a small percentage of the population crosses the axis diagonally (D/S or S/D and C/I or I/C). Some estimates are as small as one-half of one percent for the D/S and S/D combinations and three percent for the C/I and I/C combinations.

We have found through decades of research and teaching that these graphs are best explained on their own, rather than being absorbed in more umbrella patterns. If your graph is more like these, please read your narrative on the corresponding page (Quadrants 13-16).

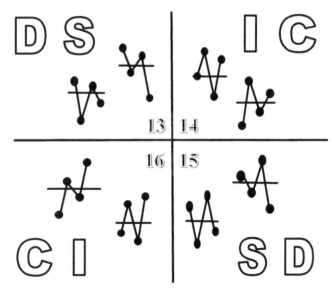

There is one more profile to consider if all four of your dimensions hover near the horizontal line.

FLATLINERS 😊

The last graph deserving its own explanation is the *Tight* or *Compressed Pattern*, or what I more fondly call *Flatliners*. No, I am not talking about people who have no personality! I am talking about people whose responses on the assessment resulted in having all four dimensions close to the horizontal line. A few examples are below. Please read narrative 17 if all four of your dimensions hover close to the line.

OVER AND UNDERS

What if your graph show four dimensions above the line or four below the line as shown in the examples below?

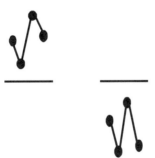

These patterns do not really exist. It is impossible to get a high score on all four traits and equally impossible to get a low score on all four traits. When participants choose an adjective that is weighted for a particular dimension, it prevents them from choosing an adjective weighted for one of the other three dimensions

Math is usually the culprit. If you have four above or below the line, take a few minutes to recount your responses. Make sure the Most column and Least column each total 24. Then make sure you correctly subtracted the *Least* column from the *Most* column to get the answer for the *Results* column (**A** column minus **B** column equals **C** column). Remember, you must have some negative numbers in the Results column as well as positive numbers.

If your math was correct, retake the assessment with a clearer focus on a specific context or role, such as work, home, school, or church.

DISC-17©

PROFILE NARRATIVES

5

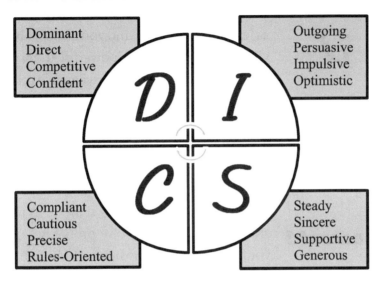

Dominant	Outgoing
Direct	Persuasive
Competitive	Impulsive
Confident	Optimistic

D *I*

C *S*

Compliant	Steady
Cautious	Sincere
Precise	Supportive
Rules-Oriented	Generous

The following narratives represent the seventeen DISC profiles identified in the preceding graphs. While we will explore the model in much more detail as the text progresses, each narrative concludes with brief suggestions for moving forward as you begin to learn more about yourself and others. Categorizing complex human behavioral preferences into only seventeen categories is obviously fraught with generalizations. The nuances and degrees with which your highs and lows fall on the graph are infinite. And remember, the instrument measures your natural response to the world, not your complete personality. For these reasons, rarely will any single narrative completely describe you.

We are looking for *patterns of behavior*. I think you will find a more than adequate level of specificity and accuracy with your profile narrative—more than enough to equip you with a much deeper understanding of both your natural responses to the world as well as those of others.

The High *D*

Quadrant 1

The High D profile represents *Dominance*. Perhaps more than anything, you value control. Whether you are ready to admit this or not, you generally view your environment as less than desirable, and you almost always view yourself as more powerful than your environment. With this convergence arises a person with a strong sense of independence and personal accountability.

Because you thrive on autonomy, you are easily demoralized in a restrictive environment. You may be so self-reliant that you often gravitate towards going it alone in many aspects of your life. You've probably said to yourself on many occasions, "I know it will get done the way I want if I do it myself." Control does not mean you are always barking orders, although commanding others to do your bidding is well within your comfort zone. Control to you may mean sitting back and watching quietly knowing you are in control or contemplating ways to gain control should the need arise.

You also value reach. It is not enough to control your immediate circumstances. You have a strong drive to grow your circumstances, to expand your influence. Sometimes your quest for greater reach manifests in strong ambition for rank and positions of authority. Sometimes it is more about informal power and influence.

You are about results, and you easily become bored. This can make life very interesting. You are much more concerned with getting the job done and moving on to the next project than getting the job done right. This is not to say you don't value a good product or want to make good decisions; it just means the product or decision doesn't have to be perfect. You would rather get ten things done at an A- level today rather than one thing at an A+ level.

You are strong-willed, independent, mission-focused, and rarely satisfied. This drives your penchant for innovation and hard work. You attack life, never waiting for things to happen. You are a doer. You not only compete with others but continuously compete with yourself. You clearly identify with the statement made by one of the greatest tennis players of our time (and another High D), Martina Navratilova: "Whoever said, 'it's not whether you win or lose that counts,' probably lost."

You believe in creating your own luck and success. As such, you thrive in new and uncharted territories and can be counted on as an innovative and dynamic force in whatever context you find yourself. You are a problem solver. Not one to mince words or avoid conflict, you are direct and clear with your communications. You thrive under stress and tight deadlines. You are decisive and comfortable with high degrees of risk when making decisions.

The growth areas of this profile also are prevalent. Because you can be so self-reliant, you may not rely on the wisdom of others to influence your decision making. Indeed, you often need to experience failure even when others have counseled, warned, or begged you to make a different decision. You can be very judgmental—and your judgments are often rooted in what *you* see of value as opposed to what others or the organization view as important.

Patience is not your virtue and for good reason. You detest procrastination and avoidance of work. You despise it in yourself and others, and you do not tolerate incompetence. While failure may be your deepest fear, your quickest trigger to anger is to be taken advantage of—and your perception of that is all that matters. This results-oriented, impatient style often projects a "my way or the highway" persona, which may lead to communication and conflict challenges as people may see you as too domineering, abrasive, unempathetic, and even obnoxious at times.

Moving Forward: Of all your strengths, as with the High I, S, and C profiles, balance may be your single most important growth opportunity. Any strength overused may become a liability. Developing balance in your behavior requires changes in your perceptions of the world around you. Recognize that not all contexts are hostile or unfriendly. Tone down the need for control in every aspect of your life. It is okay to be a follower from time to time.

Your desire for control coupled with a results-orientated mindset may affect your capacity to delegate. Some High D profiles are weak in this area, choosing to do most things themselves. However, the savvy High Ds know the best and quickest results are usually accomplished through teams, making them exceptional delegators. These savvy High Ds take the time to teach and coach, and they empower their followers to make decisions.

Yet, even the practical High Ds still do not tolerate incompetence, procrastination, or perceived inadequacies of any kind. Impatience and even a strong temper often result. Micromanaging may be a problem. Work on your delegation skills if this is a growth area for you.

You view rules as guidelines or suggestions (unless they are *your* rules). This is exactly the type of behavior that gets things done and probably in unique and ambitious ways. However, rules are usually in place for a reason. Disregarding them at leisure will ultimately lead to failure and certainly alienate those around you who believe in following rules.

You need to stay busy, always moving and doing something. You may even judge your self-worth on what you get accomplished today. Under pressure, you usually rid yourself of stress through ranting and challenging others. Conflict seems to calm your inner self. In a fight-or-flight scenario, you almost always fight. As a result, other profiles may feel intimidated or unnecessarily controlled. Consider taking time to relax a little, even during stressful times. It will help you as well as those around you.

Recognize the need for others, the value of teams and alliances, in accomplishing great things. Remember what Vince Lombardi offered: "Individual commitment to a group effort: That is what makes a team work, a company work, a society work, a civilization work."

Work on displaying a sense of caring for others. I am not suggesting to a High D that you need to suddenly become warm and fuzzy. I am only observing that people need to know you care about them, particularly if you are in a leadership role. Asking questions and actively listening will help demonstrate how much you value the people around you. Be careful in your communications, particularly with High S profiles. You may come across as pushy, aggressive, and overpowering.

Each of us needs to behave in all four DISC dimensions throughout the day depending on the needs of the situation. Work on recognizing when and how to elevate the power of the other three dimensions when it's justified by the people or situation around you.

The High I

Quadrant 2

The High I profile represents *Influence*. You almost always view your surroundings as friendly and yourself in control. Your control is informed through exceptional communication skills. With D, S, and C dimensions below the line, you are *all* about people. Whether in small groups or the largest of crowds, you thrive in contexts where you can engage with others, where you are able to express your thoughts, ideas, and opinions.

But expression is not enough. You want (need) to pull people towards your vision. And you have plenty of vision. Of all four umbrella dimensions, you are the most visionary, always looking to the future in exciting and inspiring ways. Whether in personal relationships, work environment, or even in most settings, you are the one with the positive attitude, persuasive capabilities, enthusiasm, and confidence moving the conversation and people forward.

Because you're people-oriented, you place a significant emphasis on building relationships. In the work setting, you are all about networking within and outside the organization. You know your kid's teachers by first name. At home, you know all the neighbors, and they all know you. After all, you are fun to be around because you carry conversations in otherwise awkward settings. You entertain people with your quick wit, humor, and charm. Your enthusiasm for life and all things possible is contagious. You inspire people and you make people feel good about themselves. You also tend to show more tolerance across many areas of humanity, from behavior and insights to demographics such as religion, race, and cultural differences. Your zest for life is powerful. It is almost palpable in the eyes of those around you. You are an idea person, always challenging yourself and others with new and exciting possibilities for the future.

Along with the three other profiles with one dimension above the line, you have areas that could stand some improvement. Prestige and status are of high value to you. What people around you may not know is that your motives can be ego-driven, and manipulation is your tool of persuasion.

You don't just want people to believe in what you are selling because it is a great idea or product, you want them to believe in *you*. Your ego requires it, and public humiliation, lack of inclusion, and loss of social acceptance may be your greatest fears. Your emotions are a powerful tool in winning friends and building relationships, but they often emerge unrestrained and even animated.

Your focus on people means you have less focus on things. Planning, organization, and details are not your friends. This convergence often means you still value success and attaining goals, but the excitement of the idea and the journey you take with others are much more important to you than the goal itself.

Moving Forward: As with the High D, S, and C profiles, balance may be your single most important growth opportunity. Remember, any strength overused may become a liability. Spontaneity is a good example. Your inclination for impulsive behavior can be inspiring and exciting but overused; it can lead down a path of disorganization and procrastination. Your playfulness is entertaining and lightens otherwise heavy or boring situations, but timing is everything. Some High I profiles have difficulty knowing the difference between fun time and game time.

Similarly, in your efforts to inspire and make people feel good about themselves, you can overuse praise. Praise is a wonderful thing, but use it accurately and judiciously, or it will lose its power and may make you appear insincere and superficial. Developing balance in your behavior requires changes in your perceptions of the world around you. Recognize there are times where your strength of personality will not carry the day. This acceptance may help you better prepare for tasks instead of relying on your charm, quick intellect, and *gift of gab*.

Larger-than-life personalities like you can sometimes use people to suit your own needs at the expense of theirs. If you recognize that you are using people this way, try harder to see them as separate entities with their own agendas.

Give some thought to overextending yourself. Because of your deep optimism, need for constant challenge, and desire to make people happy, you tend to overcommit beyond either your capabilities or time constraints. Time management is often a challenge for you.

You love being around people, and you are a talker. Work on your listening skills if this is a growth area for you. It will empower others and better ingratiate them to your cause. Consider giving others the center of attention, allowing them to freely express themselves without interruption. You need the energy and social acceptance provided by expressing yourself, but occasionally, it's okay to be quiet (and as my wife says, "Give others a break!").

Each of us needs to behave in all four DISC dimensions throughout the day depending on the needs of the situation. Work on recognizing when and how to elevate the power of the other three dimensions when dictated by the people or situation around you.

The
High
S

Quadrant 3

The High **S** profile represents *steadiness* and *sincerity*. You almost always view your surroundings as positive but often feel less powerful than those surroundings. This may be one of the reasons you display such a high level of respect for others.

You are dependable, considerate, and generous. You love helping others. You are a team player embracing collaboration and cooperation. In fact, just as your High I friends, you need the social acceptance of your friends and coworkers. And just as you give sincere praise to others, you want that from them.

Many consider you shy and introverted. However, this really depends on the situation. In small, comfortable groups of friends and coworkers, you are very outgoing, very chatty at times. But in large settings, you may become very quiet, often clinging to a friend or loved one for security. You are not scared in these settings, just a little apprehensive and uncomfortable.

You are everyone's friend because of your sincere, supportive, and caring attitude. You care more about others than yourself, so you tend to be a great listener. You have a sense of modesty about you that endears you quickly to others. With no hidden agenda and such a deep-rooted genuineness, you make people feel comfortable and non-threatened in your presence. People trust you.

But you still have growth opportunities ahead of you just as your High D, I, and C friends. High S profiles can be possessive at times. This occasionally manifests with objects if you view something as a source of security (e.g., the proverbial child's blankie). More often, the possessiveness presents with people. You prefer smaller, informal groups, so friendships mean a lot to you. You may become resentful if you perceive others intruding on those relationships or if close friends start paying more attention to others. Though the possessive nature of the High S seems to lessen with age and wisdom, continue to beware of this tendency even into your older years.

Your sense of loyalty is admirably strong, but it may overshadow the flaws, misjudgments, and poor decisions of those around you. This strong loyalty, almost blind at times, coupled with an innate aversion to conflict and confrontation, presents a dynamic where you may avoid holding people accountable.

You are a patient, steady, and calming voice throughout the day. Yet, crisis can change this very quickly. You tend to be resistant to change and need time to adapt to new and dynamic environments. High D and C profiles see life in clear black and white contrasts. You view life more as a gray area, often seeing the benefits of both sides of an issue. While this optimistic and objective lens can be beneficial, it also may lead to indecision and over-accommodation. Most of the time, you are happy and content—another reason everyone loves a High S. The challenge is that contentment leads to a proclivity for status quo. Innovation and risk-taking are not characteristics you embrace easily.

Moving Forward: As with the High D, I, and C profiles, balance may be your single most important growth opportunity. Because you view your surroundings as more powerful, you typically do not embrace conflict unless your back is against the wall—peace and harmony are your comfort zones. This may appear to those around you as submission, weakness, or insecurity, which can lead to being perceived as ineffective in your leadership roles or someone taking advantage of you. Work on your confidence. Train yourself to feel strong and empowered in otherwise-seeming environments.

Work on your conflict skills, particularly in your leadership roles (supervisor, parent, coach). You are a kind and sincere person, so you are generally very adept at brokering peace. But remember, leaders do not avoid conflict or try to crush it. There are times you need to embrace conflict in a constructive manner. Managing healthy conflict is good for your tribe (home, work, teams) and good for you as an individual.

Because you do not want to hurt anyone's feelings or be seen as the bad guy, you tend to be more indirect in your communications, often taking a softer approach to difficult conversations. Certainly, there is a time and place for tact and the more lenient approach, but work on being clearer and more direct in your communications, particularly when you are in a leadership position.

Because you are all about people, you spend less time focused on things. Avoid procrastination. Learn to balance the people and things in your life. And yes, your humility ingratiates you with everyone. But remember there are times when the people around you want, even need, to see confidence and decisiveness in your approach.

Each of us needs to behave in all four DISC dimensions throughout the day depending on the needs of the situation. Work on recognizing when and how to elevate the power of the other three dimensions when dictated by the people or situations around you.

The High C

Quadrant 4

With D, I, and S dimensions below the line, the High C profile represents *compliance* above all. You like to follow the rules. Rules give you a sense of security, control, predictability, and organization amidst the chaos of the world. As your gravitation towards conformity extends to people, you rarely challenge authority unless those in power are violating the rules, policies, or accepted social norms. Usually reserved and not prone to confrontation, you can become a fierce fighter in these situations.

You are a critical thinker, strongly valuing accuracy, details, and facts. You need to understand the way things work at what others may consider a micro level. Because of your analytical nature and need to get things right, you place great emphasis on meticulous planning. You have often echoed the old saying, "If it's worth doing, it's worth doing right."

You are self-disciplined and deliberate in thought and deed. You are focused. You have the ability to block out distractions better than most people. When immersed in a project, you may not even hear those around you talking, the TV, phone, or even an ambulance siren. You are a hard worker. You are no quitter. In fact, you can be absolutely dogged in your quest to learn, build, and lead.

You are precise in your actions and words and expect the same of others. While DISC does not measure values, beliefs, and character, you do tend to be honest because otherwise would be breaking societal rules and expectations. People who exaggerate, lie, and even use large generalizations in their speech highly frustrate you.

In fact, people in general often frustrate you. You may even consider yourself socially awkward, often avoiding social interaction. You certainly value family and close friendships, but most of the time you are completely comfortable alone. Indeed, too much interaction with people drains you of energy—the classic introvert.

Because you highly value correctness, you need time to complete your tasks. Short deadlines and last-minute challenges are strong demotivators for you. You want perfection, and nothing perfect happens without the time to plan and analyze every consideration and consequence. You are normally reserved in your emotions and let the facts speak for themselves. However, you can become irate, even insubordinate, when you believe unrealistic expectations and time restraints are thrust upon you.

You can be shy and subdued, particularly in environments you view as unfriendly. The environment does not have to be hostile, as in shots fired or the building burning down. It may be something as seemingly innocuous as being at your spouse's work party, an event you've dreaded for weeks. It could be you have not had much sleep lately, so you will perceive no environment as friendly. It simply could be the weather. Rainy Monday mornings generally do not put many people in good moods.

Moving Forward: As with the High D, I, and S profiles, balance may be your single most important growth opportunity. Strong critical thinking skills help define your lens of the world and subsequent response to it. But any skill overused may become a liability. Your need to critically analyze every aspect of a decision may lead to what is referred to as *analysis paralysis,* which can create a situation where you get so bogged down in the scrutiny of the issues the decision never gets made.

Jeff Boss suggested several considerations to improve in this area. Set a drop-dead time for your projects and decisions. Recognize that the moons will *never* align exactly—and perfection doesn't always have to be the end goal. Curb your inclination to dig deeper into every aspect of the situation, follow every new detail that arises, and explore every hypothetical consequence. Establishing parameters for what you truly need to know as opposed to what you would like to know will help mitigate what appears to many as procrastination or indecision.

Because you generally view your surroundings as unfriendly, you sometimes portray a sense of pessimism. Most people want to buy into a bright future and they want to be around those who inspire them with their optimism and enthusiasm. The last thing anyone wants to hear when they think they have a great idea is, "It won't work because . . . ."

If this is a growth area for you, consider framing your perspective and response along the lines of, "Your idea may be difficult for a variety of reasons, but no great accomplishments were ever easy. Let's think this through together, and figure how to overcome some apparent obstacles as we go forward." With this altered view, you still retain the skepticism of your inner wiring but offer a path forward if that person is willing to work hard and meet reality head-on.

Given your propensity towards things as opposed to people, give some thought to your communication and conflict skills. You win most arguments on merit because you almost always know the policies and stats better than your opponent. But winning is a subjective concept. High Ds care little for rules and facts. Unless they made the rules, they quite often look at them as barriers to accomplishing what needs to be done. High I's value the argument itself because it a time for them to engage and persuade others to their cause. They may value intangibles (vision, dreams, ideals) much more than your facts, and they may even win others to their cause because of their contagious rhetoric. You could win the battle but lose the war.

Give some consideration to the notion that other personalities may not connect with your position just because facts and figures are on your side. Each of us needs to behave in all four DISC dimensions throughout the day depending on the needs of the situation. Work on recognizing when and how to elevate the power of the other three dimensions as the people or situation around you dictate.

The

D/C

Quadrant 5

The D/C combination represents D and C dimensions above the line with S and I below the line. We all are a blend of all four dimensions, and the D/C profile behaves primarily with D tendencies and secondarily with C tendencies. Fluctuating between the two dimensions may appear both seamless or abrupt at times. You often act neither as a pure D nor pure C due to the thorough blending of the two dominant dimensions (and the two below the line), creating a profile that is unique in itself.

You are persistent and results-driven. The D in you is active, almost aggressive in your approach to life. The C is about perfection, accuracy, and intellectual curiosity. You may best be characterized as someone who wants things done your way, and they need to be done right.

You are self-disciplined, deliberate, and focused. You can block out distractions better than most people. When immersed in a project, you may not even hear those around you talking, the TV or the phone, or even a siren outside. You are a hard worker. You are no quitter. In fact, you can be absolutely dogged in your quest to learn, build, and lead.

Often the loner, you seldom seek advice from other people. When you do, you ask sharp questions, even if they're unpopular. You prefer to learn and create through trial and error, or you study alone. You will work with others, particularly as you have matured over the years, but you still would rather work alone. You frustrate easily when you have to wait on others to do their part, and frankly, you do not like to share control.

You are highly critical of both yourself and others, with a

tendency to correct people when they make mistakes, even to the point of highlighting errors they may view as minor and inconsequential. Your bluntness is sometimes perceived as fresh and honest with no hidden agenda, and sometimes perceived as insensitive, condescending, and even self-righteous. You can be skeptical of people's motives and sometimes prefer not to share information unless absolutely necessary. When communication with others is essential, you tend to be clear and concise, focusing on practical issues and tasks.

You sometimes struggle with delegation when in a leadership role, although you clearly recognize its value. There is not enough time in the day for you to do everything you want to get accomplished. You know delegation is the only path, yet your propensity to *go it alone* can get in the way. When you do delegate, you can be clear in your communication and precise with the instructions. Yet, you also can micromanage and become very critical when things do not progress in the time or way you deem appropriate. You believe in getting things done right and rarely are afraid to state your position vigorously and directly.

Willpower abounds in your approach to tasks. You are dogged, determined and have strong opinions. People who know you best probably have expressed their observation that you indeed relish conflict. The D is about power: *Do it because I said so. I am the boss. I am in control.* The C is about compliance: *Do it because the rules say so. I have the rules in writing. I am the expert in this field.* Influenced by the D and C dimensions, you are not easily deterred once you make a decision.

You do experience internal conflict depending on how you view your level of control in relation to your environment. When you feel more powerful, you choose between options quickly, often demonstrating extraordinary decisiveness on one hand or uninformed impulse on the other. When you feel less powerful than your environment, you will take time making decisions while deliberating as many considerations and consequences, intended and unintended, as possible.

Your desire for rapid success is counterbalanced by an equally strong drive for precision, just as your forcefulness is often tempered by your conscientiousness. Perhaps your greatest conflict arises out of your primary need for change and challenge, tempered by your secondary inclination towards rules, policies, and security—the status quo. As stark as these conflicts appear, you handle them quite smoothly, often segueing effortlessly between them as your perception of your power changes throughout the day. We will discuss this notion of power and environment in depth later in the text.

Please read both the High D (Quadrant 1) and High C (Quadrant 4) narratives in the beginning of this chapter. See if some of the strengths and growth areas of both profiles resonate with you, and then consider the applicable suggestions for growth offered in the *Moving Forward* narratives.

The

D/I

Quadrant 6

The D/I profile represents D and I dimensions above the line with S and C below the line. We all are a blend of all four dimensions, but the D/I profile behaves primarily with D tendencies and secondarily with I tendencies. Fluctuating between the two dimensions may appear seamless or abrupt at times. You often act neither as a pure D nor pure I due to the thorough blending of the two dimensions (and the two below the line), creating a profile that is unique in itself.

A good example is your ability to flow smoothly between people and things. While you are mission-driven first, you value the journey and the relationships made along the way. You recognize the surest and quickest path to task achievement is through strong leadership founded in credibility and trust with those around you.

Accurately or not, you almost always view yourself as more powerful than your environment. How you view your circumstances at a specific instance usually determines your behavior (we will address the notion of power and environment more in Chapter 6). For example, persistence and a competitive spirit define you. You go through life at a face pace looking for new challenges and new opportunities—always willing to stretch routine and accepted boundaries. How you succeed often may fluctuate between behaviors consistent with either the D or I dimension. When you view the environment as unfavorable, the D dimension emergences with power and dominance. When you view your environment as favorable, the I dimension emerges, using persuasion, manipulation, and your strong communication skills to succeed.

As with all combination profiles, you sometimes do the same thing but for different motives. For instance, you occasionally give your office a pretty good cleaning and straightening—nothing too over the top, but a decent job. The D in you does it because you cannot seem to get anything accomplished when the clutter gets unruly. The I dimension does it because someone might come in and judge you negatively on the way things look. With D and I above the line, you may fluctuate between both motives, or perhaps both motives inform your decision to straighten things.

Appearances matter to you. The D in you works hard, and it is often important to you that others recognize this. You hold yourself to a strong work ethic and you expect no less of those around you regardless of the context. The I in you is creative, moving forward with zeal and enthusiasm. The High I wants recognition for this too—partly because I profiles like the attention but partly because you need to persuade others to your side of whatever the issue is at the time.

With your energy, drive, and impulsive propensities, you want things to happen *now*. Your sense of urgency is unsurpassed. When things do not happen at the pace you want, you can become annoyed, impatient, and even harsh in word and action. You will attempt to persuade and motivate those around you to get the job done, but if that does not work, your default is force and dominance. You are not afraid to make demands of others, regardless of their rank or position or their needs. Informed by both the D and I dimensions, you also are quite adept at using words to hurt people. You almost innately sense people's vulnerabilities and have little reservations in exploiting them when you deem necessary.

You can have a great sense of humor, but it has an edge. Your typical approach at humor is direct and to the point without pulling any punches, and it may include a bit of self-importance. Your picking and poking and having fun at other's expenses is often very funny. However, not knowing where the line is or when to stop can present difficulty for you.

You are confident—sometimes too confident, even bordering on obnoxious—and lack the ability to recognize your limitations. Your self-assurance manifests not just in the way you carry yourself, but in your motives and actions as well. Your adventurous spirit needs autonomy. Restrictive environments frustrate and drain you of motivation. No task or goal is ever beyond you. You need the latitude to think big and do big. You love a big stage with big problems and big consequences. As a result, you thrive in challenge and crisis, particularly when all eyes are on you for success.

You are a thinker and a doer. Your supervisors, peers, subordinates, family, and friends often look to you to make things happen. Your enthusiasm energizes people, while your dominance can intimidate and alienate at times. You have the uncanny ability to both draw people in and distance them at the same time. Read both the High D (Quadrant 1) and High I (Quadrant 2) narratives in the beginning of this chapter. See if some of the strengths and growth areas of both profiles resonate with you and then consider the applicable suggestions for growth offered in the *Moving Forward* narratives.

The

I/D

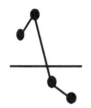

Quadrant 7

The I/D profile represents I and D dimensions above the line with S and C below the line. We all are a blend of all four dimensions, but the I/D profile behaves primarily with I tendencies and secondarily with D tendencies. As with D/I profiles, fluctuating between the two dimensions often appears seamless, and it also can appear sudden. One minute you are playful and the life of the party. The next minute you abruptly tell your spouse it is time to leave. Many times in your life you have probably heard, "What just flipped your switch?"

You often act neither as a pure I nor pure D due to the thorough blending of the two dimensions (plus the two below the line), creating a profile that is unique in itself. Your primary dimension focuses on people while your secondary focuses on tasks. However, you may bring both dimensions to bear in the same instance.

Let's say you are having difficulty getting buy-in from one of your employees on a new priority program. While persuasion is still your tool of choice, you will use it with a sense of urgency, clarity, and force uncommon to those with only the I dimension above the line. Another example is your sense of trust. The I profile is very trusting. The D profile trusts little. The I/D trusts but verifies.

You are adept at using people's intrinsic needs to your advantage. You give friendship to those looking for acceptance. You empower those who need control. You provide security to those who crave status quo. You ask people questions about themselves, demonstrating, at least ostensibly, how much you value them. All the while, however, you continue to push and pull to bring people to your side, to win them over. Your emotional intelligence is sky-high, but your commitment to truly caring about people fluctuates depending on all sorts of variables.

As with the D/I profile, you are confident—sometimes too confident, biting off more than you can handle. Your self-assurance manifests not just in the way you carry yourself, but in your motives and actions as well. You value both prestige and power, seeking to maintain a position of control throughout the day regardless of the context. You want to be both liked and respected by those around you.

Your ability to captivate an audience, persuade a group of people to your side, or inspire an entire organization or cause has made you successful time and again. Because of this, you often do not take the appropriate time to plan and prepare. Charisma can be your trap unless you take time to equally build your substance.

Your outgoing tendencies include fun and humor, but usually with an edge. Your typical approach at humor is direct and to the point without pulling any punches and may include a bit of self-importance and a way for you to take center stage. Your self-deprecating humor, as well as your picking, poking, and having fun at other's expenses, is often very funny. However, knowing where the line is or when to stop can be difficult for you.

You need autonomy and challenge—both the I and D dimensions frustrate easily and lose self-motivation in boring and restrictive environments. No task or goal is ever beyond you. You need the latitude to think big and do big. You love a big stage with big problems and big consequences. As a result, you thrive in challenge and crisis, particularly when all eyes are on you for success. Your big-picture view of life is powerfully inspiring. Remember, though, when you always look only at the forest, you never see the individual trees. This may be a growth area for you regarding people and goals.

You are a thinker and a doer. You are good at selling and closing the deal. Your supervisors, peers, subordinates, family, and friends often look to you to make things happen. While you are people-oriented first, you value the accomplishment of the goal and will resort to force or over-persuasion if necessary. Your enthusiasm energizes people, but your dominance can intimidate and alienate at times. You are capable of dynamic action or charming affability depending on the needs of the circumstances. You have the uncanny ability to both draw people in and distance them all at the same time. You possess clear goals in life with the resolve and commitment to accomplish them.

Please read both the High I (Quadrant 2) and High D (Quadrant 1) narratives in the beginning of this chapter. See if some of the strengths and growth areas of both profiles resonate with you, and then consider the applicable suggestions for growth offered in the *Moving Forward* narratives.

The I/S profile represents I and S dimensions above the line with D and C below the line. We all are a blend of all four dimensions, but the I/S profile behaves primarily with I tendencies and secondarily with S tendencies. The I/S profile is all about people.

The

I/S

Quadrant 8

Both the I and S dimensions are more oriented towards feelings and emotions than things. The High S dimension cares about people while the High I dimension has an intellectual and emotional need to understand them. Taken together, the I/S is confident, outgoing, friendly, inquisitive, and empathetic. You are helpful and patient and often willing to compromise as a result. As Will Rogers offered, "Strangers are just people I haven't met yet." You seem to wear a smile on your face more than all other profiles.

You do experience conflict, as do all the other combination profiles. However, you are very adept at fluctuating between your two high dimensions smoothly and seamlessly, as it seems to most people. Your orientation towards people over things changes little throughout the day. What does change, however, is your approach—more assertive or more passive, all driven by how you perceive yourself in relation to your environment in that instant—more powerful or less powerful accordingly. The I dimension almost attacks life with risk-taking, vision, and lofty dreams. The S dimension is more reserved, content, and appreciative of security and status quo. Your High I dimension likes to be in charge, while your High S dimension is comfortable in supporting roles. You have the capacity to flow between both sides of the same coin almost effortlessly.

Much of the time, you don't act quite as an I or quite as an S, as the thorough blending together of the two top dimensions (and the two below the line) creates a profile that is unique in itself. For instance, you have a colleague who is not quite on board with your vision. You will spend an inordinate amount of time and energy selling your ideas to that person. Your High D colleague would have told him weeks ago *get on board or jump ship*. Your action is consistent with the High I's need to persuade and win others over, but the inordinate amount of time with just one person is much more consistent with the High S dimension. The I/S profile emerges as a blending of the two.

Charming, sincere, and engaging, you are viewed as the great communicator. Your I dimension is spontaneous and confident allowing you to comfortably speak to the masses while relishing in the spotlight. Your S dimension loves engaging in more trusting and secure smaller groups with friends, family, and coworkers. Regardless of the context, you can be depended upon to carry the conversation.

Because you are so forward-looking and highly oriented towards people, you may often neglect tasks. Regardless of how strong your work ethic, you may find difficulty pulling away from conversations that are draining you of the time needed to complete your tasks. You need human connectivity, and you do not want to hurt anyone's feelings. You generally do not miss a deadline, but you do not often beat deadlines, either.

For the same reasons you sometimes neglect tasks, you also sometimes neglect the facts. You tend to speak in the narrative with more vagueness and generalizations than other profiles. "They've done studies on this." The High C cringes at such statements. Who are *they*? What *studies*? DISC does not measure integrity and character, so don't take offense to this: You may exaggerate or over-generalize from time to time, and you certainly don't want the facts to get in the way of a good story.

Because the I/S profile is so focused on people, people affect you more than they do other profiles. You constantly are in observation mode, scanning people's words, deeds, and non-verbal cues to gain a nuanced sense of their sincerity and commitment. When life is good, filled with social acceptance and praise, you are energetic, enthusiastic, and happy. On the other hand, when you perceive strong confrontation or a loss of social acceptance or friendship, your energy drains, your motivation fades, and your mood turns to sadness and rejection. Just as you are so adept at making people feel good about themselves, you too need to feel that you are appreciated, respected, and liked by the people around you.

Please read both the High I (Quadrant 2) and High S (Quadrant 3) narratives in the beginning of this chapter. See if some of the strengths and growth areas of both profiles resonate with you and then consider the applicable suggestions for growth offered in the *Moving Forward* narratives.

The
S/I

Quadrant 9

The S/I profile represents S and I dimensions above the line with D and C below the line. We all are a blend of all four dimensions, but the S/I profile behaves primarily with S tendencies and secondarily with I tendencies. As with your I/S friends, the S/I profile is all about people.

Both the S and I dimensions are more oriented towards feelings and emotions than things. The high S dimension cares about feelings while the high I dimension has an intellectual and emotional need to understand people. Taken together, the S/I profile is thoughtful, welcoming, sympathetic, and inquisitive. You wear a smile on your face with a genuine sense of friendliness and contentment. You likely spend a great deal of your time making new relationships and working on existing ones.

With S as your highest dimension, you are a good listener and not afraid to consider other people's opinions and ideas. You understand the tremendous value in establishing and maintaining trusting relationships. You know the most powerful way to show people you care is to spend time with them. You ask questions demonstrating your concern and also help them with problems.

The I dimension likes attention for its own sake, but you are adept at tempering that pull and letting others have the attention and space. Because of this, people are drawn to you, particularly in times of need. Your easy-going persona presents warmth, comfort, and acceptance. Some days it seems as if you cannot get any work done because people keep talking to you.

Everyone wants to tell you their story. Everyone trusts you. Everyone wants to be your friend.

Your soft-spoken friendliness and compassion towards people may be your most endearing qualities. However, when not managed properly, those characteristics can lead to the outright avoidance of conflict and high-pressure situations. They can lead to a lack of assertiveness, clarity in words and tone in tough conversations, and objectivity. Your patience and loyalty, especially with friends, can be a blind spot, pushing you to sometimes focus more on the virtues of a person rather than the constructive criticism of their performance.

You do experience conflict, as with the other combination profiles. However, you are very adept at fluctuating between your two high dimensions in a seamless fashion. Your orientation towards people over tasks changes little throughout the day. What does change, however, is your approach—more assertive or more passive, all driven by how you perceive yourself in relation to your environment in that instant—more powerful or less powerful accordingly (we will discuss this notion of power and environment in chapter 6).

The S dimension is more reserved, satisfied, and appreciative of stability and status quo. The I dimension ambitiously tackles life with grand visions and risk-taking. You have the capacity to flow between both sides of the same coin almost effortlessly.

Because your profile with S and I above the line is about people, people affect you more than they do those with other profiles. You tend to feel emotional highs and lows more often and easier than others do. When life is good with social acceptance and appreciation, you are energetic, enthusiastic, and happy. However, when you perceive strong confrontation or a loss of social acceptance or friendship, your energy drains, your motivation fades, and your mood turns to sadness and rejection.

You are keenly aware how your words and deeds make others feel and are sensitive enough to alter them when necessary. You project sincerity and sensitivity, and you internalize those characteristics just as deeply. Just as you are so adept at making people feel good about themselves, you too need to feel that you are appreciated, respected, and liked by the people around you.

You are great at bringing people together. You know the best way to communicate is to get others to engage with one another. Your listening skills and diplomatic, friendly approach make you the ideal team member. In fact, you are adept at assembling individuals into functioning teams that respect both results and the journey to accomplish them.

Please read both the High S (Quadrant 3) and High I (Quadrant 2) narratives in the beginning of this chapter. See if some of the strengths and growth areas of both profiles resonate with you and then consider the applicable suggestions for growth offered in the *Moving Forward* narratives.

The
S/C

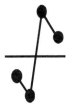

Quadrant 10

The S/C profile represents S and C dimensions above the line with I and D below the line. We all are a blend of all four dimensions, but the S/C profile behaves primarily with S tendencies and secondarily with C tendencies. The High S is about people while the High C is about tasks. Taken together, you get things done and done right the first time.

Driven by both the S and C dimensions, you approach life at a more patient and slower pace than most other profiles. Because of your even temperament, fair-minded approach, and caring attitude (High S dimension), you need time to consider all sides of issues and ensure everyone's feelings are considered. Your propensity towards accuracy and quality (High C dimension) requires time to plan, prepare, and accomplish your tasks correctly the first time. As a result, time management may be a struggle, particularly with stressful and seemingly overwhelming demands made on you.

Even if you do not voice it, you resent others for pushing you for quicker results. You move through life best at your own pace, free from outside stressors. In fact, your orientation to people can be a stressor. When you're trying to accomplish something, particularly a task with a looming deadline, people represent a huge distraction since your instinct is to give them attention instead of working on the task. For the most part, you do not miss deadlines or time tables, but you rarely beat them with a lot of time to spare. You are consistent and stable, always with an eye towards quality.

Among your most endearing characteristics, you are sincere,

genuine, caring, and loyal. Your humility and deference to others separate you from other profiles. You have no hidden agenda. You are slow to anger. People feel comfortable around you. They trust you. They want to be your friend. They can count on you to maintain composure in stressful situations and offer support and comfort in times of need.

Just as people enjoy your company, you need their company as well. Even with your predisposition for details and facts, you are people-oriented first and foremost. You are sensitive to the needs of others, and you want that same acceptance and support in return. Your feelings may be hurt more easily than other profiles, but the High C in you eventually processes the details of those feelings and surrounding events, enabling you to move beyond those initial sensitivities. The High C is very capable of holding grudges, especially with people outside your network of close friends and family, but usually your S dimension prevails with forgiveness and acceptance.

Your High S dimension indicates a need for harmony, security, and stability. Chaos and tense environments are not your friends. Your High C is about compliance with the rules, regulations, and even social expectations. Both dimensions favor status quo and contentment. These inclinations provide a stable and dependable environment for those around you. However, they may lead to a lack of initiative as well as risk aversion, inflexibility, and an overabundance of caution. Unlike your High I and D friends, you live more in the present as opposed to big-picture future initiatives fraught with risk and danger. When you do consider the future, you like it as planned, secured, and settled as much as possible.

You are persistent but may need a little nudging or direction to get started down a particular path. Once you get started, there is no stopping you. However, your persistence, unchecked, may turn to stubbornness. Once your mind is made up, it is very hard to change. You have the capacity to alter your decisions if you deliberately open your mind to new ideas, approaches, and, of course, evidence supporting a different path.

You are generally open in your communications and approach with others. You can be quite talkative in small groups of friends and family, but are often quiet and reserved in large groups, particularly in settings where you do not know people. Your openness also has limitations in situations where you perceive that openness will hurt those around you. It causes you pain to hurt other's feelings, especially those close to you. You are keenly aware how your words and deeds make others feel and are sensitive enough to alter them when necessary.

Your compassion, along with your sense of modesty and need for social acceptance, often manifests in difficulty with conflict. You can be overly reticent to challenge others when you disagree with their position or even when you believe you are being exploited. This may appear to others that you possess a high level of agreeableness. As you well know, though much of the time that's correct, people should not assume you agree just because you haven't challenged their decisions.

A potential growth opportunity may be to work on your ability to confront people in appropriate circumstances. Your natural diplomatic and friendly approach will equip you well.

Please read both the High S (Quadrant 3) and High C (Quadrant 4) narratives in the beginning of this chapter. See if some of the strengths and growth areas of both profiles resonate with you, and then consider the applicable suggestions for growth offered in the *Moving Forward* narratives

The

C/S

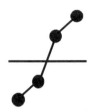

Quadrant 11

The C/S profile represents C and S dimensions above the line with D and I below the line. We all are a blend of all four dimensions, but the C/S profile behaves primarily with C tendencies and secondarily with S tendencies. Like your S/C friends and colleagues, you both have S and C dimensions above the line. Thus, you will share many behavioral similarities. But with your C higher than the S, your focus on people will, more often than not, give way to a focus on task and results.

Your High C cares about getting things done and honoring commitments, while your High S cares about people. At your worst, you may be viewed as rigid and caring more about rules, processes, and tasks than the people around you. When you are at your best, perfectly blending the strengths of the C and S dimensions, you are among the most conscientious of all profiles.

While the High C dimension is comfortable *going it alone*, the blending of your C and S results in someone who does find value in being part of the team. You expect clarity, transparency, and clear expectations of individual team members as well as the team as a whole. An ambiguous assembly of people is not a team. As reserved and unemotional as you may seem (sometimes even appearing insensitive), you often want social acceptance and reassurance from those on the team or in your circle of friends and family.

You are a critical thinker, strongly valuing precision and facts. You need to understand the way things work at what some would consider a micro level. Indeed, your D and I coworkers may sometimes accuse you of getting too buried in the minutia of a task, yet all the while they appreciate you're the one who can be counted on to know the rules, focus the team with careful deliberation, and get things done right the first time.

Because of your analytical nature and high value on quality, you place great emphasis on thorough planning and organization, particularly understanding the expectations and requirements of the task. You do not like to be wrong. Even more, you do not like to be told you are wrong. Working towards being less tense and defensive in the face of criticism may be a growth opportunity for you.

You need time to complete your tasks. Short deadlines and last-minute challenges are often strong demotivators for you. You want perfection, and nothing perfect happens without the time to plan and analyze every consideration and consequence. You also are tenacious and resolute but may need a subtle push from time to time to get out of the weeds of a task and see the big picture. Your tenacity may lead to stubbornness, making it difficult to change your mind, particularly when your opponent is countering with an emotional argument. Driven by facts and evidence, you need more than eloquent and inspirational verbiage to sway you.

You are normally reserved in your emotions and communications, often letting the facts speak for themselves. In fact, it is within your comfort zone to spend much of your time alone, even to the point of becoming isolated from others. You do enjoy the company of a coworker, friend, or family member but not so much for idle chat. Your favorite conversations often center around the details of an issue and offer a platform where you can share your knowledge or learn something new from the other person.

While you dislike conflict and are usually diplomatic in your communications, you can become irritated, even contentious, when what you perceive as unrealistic expectations and time restraints are thrust upon you. You do not like uncertainty. You frustrate more easily than most profiles when those around you ignore the rules or make up their own. Because of your self-control and discipline, it disturbs you when others fail to plan appropriately. High I profiles who like to *wing it* (and often succeed) leave you speechless.

Your High C is about compliance with rules, protocols, and even societal expectations. Your High S indicates harmony, security, and stability. Both dimensions favor status quo and contentment, and provide a stable, reliable, and dependable environment for those around you. However, these qualities may lead to a lack of creativity and decisiveness as well as rigidity, aversion to risk, and an overabundance of caution. Confusion, disorder, and stressful environments are not your friends. Yet, in times of stress, the C/S profile (particularly if the D dimension is just below the line) may make decisions very quickly and efficiently.

Unlike the High I and D profiles, you prefer the safety and predictability of status quo as opposed to risky endeavors fraught with spontaneity, uncertainty, and peril. When you do consider the untested and unknown, you like to contemplate, to the extent possible, every conceivable scenario and potential outcome. Humble and impartial, you are always prepared, diligent, and hardworking, and will never willingly let those close to you down.

Please read both the High C (Quadrant 4) and High S (Quadrant 3) narratives in the beginning of this chapter. See if some of the strengths and growth areas of both profiles resonate with you, and then consider the applicable suggestions for growth offered in the *Moving Forward* narratives.

The

C/D

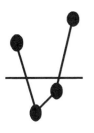

Quadrant 12

The C/D profile represents C and D dimensions above the line with I and S below the line. We all are a blend of all four dimensions, but the C/D profile behaves primarily with C tendencies and secondarily with D tendencies.

You are persistent and results-driven. The C in you is about perfection, accuracy, and intellectual curiosity. The D is active, almost zealous in your approach to life. You may be best characterized as someone who wants things done right and done in the manner of your choosing.

You are self-disciplined, deliberate, and focused. You can block out distractions better than most people. When immersed in a project, you may not even hear those around you talking, the TV or the phone, or even a siren. You are a hard worker. You are no quitter. In fact, you can be absolutely dogged in your quest to learn, build, and lead.

Often the loner, you seldom seek advice from other people. When you do, you ask sharp questions, even if unpopular. You prefer to learn and create through trial and error, or you study alone. You will work with others, particularly as you have matured over the years, but you still would rather work alone or with a close friend or associate you trust who will not consume your day with idle chat. You frustrate easily when you must wait for others to do their part, and, frankly, you do not like to share control. You are highly critical of both yourself and others, with a tendency to correct people when they make mistakes, even to the point of highlighting errors they may view as minor and inconsequential.

You do not relish confrontation, but you do not shrink from it. You are strong in your convictions and not afraid to let people know. Indeed, you often can be counted on to express contrary views, playing the role of devil's advocate and helping those around you see all sides of an issue. Your bluntness is sometimes perceived as fresh and honest with no hidden agenda. Yet, sometimes it is perceived as cold, insensitive, condescending, and even sanctimonious. You can be skeptical of people's motives and sometimes prefer not to share information unless necessary. When communication with others is essential, you tend to be clear and concise, focusing on practical issues and tasks. Small talk with no defined end does not sit well with you.

You recognize not enough time exists in the day for you to get everything you want to be accomplished if you do it alone. You know delegation is the only path, and you can be very adept at providing direction and orders. Yet, your propensity to *go it alone* can get in the way. When you delegate, you can be clear in your communication and precise with the instructions. Yet, you also can micromanage and become very critical when things do not progress in the time or way you deem appropriate. You believe in getting things done right, and rarely are afraid to offer your position forcefully and directly.

Willpower abounds in your approach to tasks. You are intensely persistent and have strong opinions. The C is about compliance: *Do it because the rules say so. I have the rules in writing. I am the expert in this field.* The D is about power: *Do it because I said so. I am the boss. I am in charge.* Influenced by both dimensions, you are not easily deterred once you make a decision, and you rarely ever quit something once you start.

Failure and lack of control are your greatest nemeses. Your tenacity may lead to stubbornness, making it difficult to change your mind, particularly when your opponent is countering with an emotional argument. Driven by facts and evidence, you need more than eloquent and inspirational verbiage to sway you.

You do experience internal conflict, depending on how you view your level of control in relation to your environment. When you feel less powerful than your environment (C dimension), you will take time making decisions while deliberating as many considerations and consequences as possible. When you feel more powerful (D dimension), you choose between options, quickly often demonstrating extraordinary decisiveness on one hand or uninformed impulse on the other.

Your desire for precision and quality is counterbalanced by an equally strong drive to accomplish things quickly, just as your conscientiousness is tempered by your assertive nature. Perhaps your greatest conflict arises out of your primary need for compliance (rules, policies, security), challenged by your secondary need for change, risk, and uncertainty. As stark as these conflicts appear, you handle them smoothly, often segueing effortlessly between them as your perceptions of your power changes throughout the day. We will discuss this notion of power and environment in depth later in the text.

Please read both the High C (Quadrant 4) and High D (Quadrant 1) narratives in the beginning of this chapter. See if some of the strengths and growth areas of both profiles resonate with you, and then consider the applicable suggestions for growth offered in the *Moving Forward* narratives.

The
D/S

Quadrant 13

The D/S profile represents D and S dimensions above the line with I and C below the line. We all are a blend of all four dimensions, but the D/S profile behaves primarily with D tendencies and secondarily with S tendencies. This profile is so rare, many instruments do not even address it. It is estimated that only one-half of one percent of the population has the D/S or S/D profile.

You often act neither as a pure D nor pure S due to the thorough blending of the two dimensions (and the two below the line), creating a profile that is unique in itself. Though your primary dimension focuses on tasks and your secondary focuses on people, you can bring both dimensions to bear at the same time. For instance, one of your employees betrays your trust. Your High D values results while your High S values loyalty. This blend of the two manifests when you hold the employee accountable for his behavior while still affording him a second chance.

You are a doer. The High D is laser-focused on results. The High S brings the worker bee ethic to the mix. Your High D is independent in nature, leading you to trust your abilities and judgment more than those of your colleagues. Your friendly and caring High S does not like to impose on others. As a result, delegation may be difficult for you even when appropriate. However, a savvy D/S has learned through trial and error that very little in life gets accomplished without relying on both self and others.

You also tend to be realistic and objective in your approach. You like to have your own space to deal with problems and tasks—a space where you can set your own timelines, pace, and approach to the extent possible. As strong as the High D can be, you still lack self-confidence on occasion. As a result, you may be a little slow to start new things, but once you do, you almost never turn back. You are genuine and transparent. The D values straightforward communication, and the S values transparency and relationships. You are equally known for your determination and willpower as well as your lack of a hidden agenda. People appreciate and respect those characteristics in you.

You generally do not like to get wrapped up in details. If necessary, you can force yourself into the weeds of an issue, but details and minutiae frustrate you. You think, *There is the goal. Let's go make it happen.* Details and preparation are obstacles, only meant to slow you down. Similarly, you appreciate structure and routine, but you easily become demoralized in a restrictive environment where you do not have a sense of control. To you, *control* does not mean barking out orders, although commanding others to do your bidding is well within your comfort zone. *Control* to you may mean sitting back and watching quietly, confident you are in control or contemplating ways to gain control should the need arise.

You can be very stubborn and opinionated, and you definitely have an independent streak. Holding your ground once a decision is made gives you the appearance of strength and conviction. When this characteristic is overused, it can lead others to see rigidity and self-righteousness. Sometimes you do enjoy a good intellectual fight, but more often than not, you will not change your mind in the end based on emotional arguments. For someone to win an argument with you, she will need crystal clear logic or factual evidence. Even then, you almost need to tangibly feel a lesson to learn from it.

While you listen to people and appear to value their interest and advice, in actuality you go through life with trial and error as your guide. Sometimes it takes two or three failures, using the same behavior in the same context, before you alter your course.

You clearly experience internal conflict, perhaps more than any other profile. You experience conflict with both how you perceive your environment (favorable or unfavorable) and how you perceive your power in relation to that environment (more powerful or less powerful). We will explore this notion of control and environment further in chapter 6. The High D is about power and control, more about results than people. The High S is about warmth and teamwork, more about people than results. Fluctuating between the two dimensions may appear smooth and seamless, or it may appear quite abrupt at times. You may be yelling one minute and apologizing the next. You also segue throughout the day from feeling more powerful than your circumstances to feeling less powerful.

You can be the domineering leader in one context and the submissive follower in the next. This explains how one moment you bark orders in full command, while in another moment you sit in the back of the room shy and reserved. A D/S friend of mine was a dominant, risk-taking, powerhouse within the walls of the business he owned. Yet, when out in public (stores, restaurants), he was cautious, subdued, even a little timid. The stark change in his behavior was bizarre to me until I learned the DISC model.

As you mature and learn to flow smoothly between the conflicting D and S dimensions, you display strength, confidence, and power balanced with fairness, loyalty, and support for those around you. Your capacity to value both results and compassion serves you well in leadership positions, supporting your people but also holding them accountable. *Tough love* may well define your approach.

Read both the High D (Quadrant 1) and High S (Quadrant 3) narratives in the beginning of this chapter. See if some of the strengths and growth areas of both profiles resonate with you and then consider the applicable suggestions for growth offered in the *Moving Forward* narratives.

The

I/C

Quadrant 14

The I/C profile represents I and C dimensions above the line with D and S below the line. We all are a blend of all four dimensions, but the I/C profile behaves primarily with I tendencies and secondarily with C tendencies. This profile is rare. Indeed, many instruments do not even address it. It is estimated that only three percent of the population has the I/C or C/I profile.

DISC is predicated on perception—how you perceive your environment (favorable or unfavorable) and how you perceive yourself in relation to that environment (less powerful or more powerful). We will talk much more about this dynamic later in the text. Your I dimension emerges when you perceive your environment as favorable. When you are happy and want to be where you are doing what you want, you are friendly and outgoing. When you perceive your environment as unfavorable (for whatever reason), your C dimension tends to take over. You become withdrawn, impatient, even critical and will focus on task over people.

You like to blend your creative ideas with pragmatism and purpose. You can be very direct but generally avoid harsh dialogue because you care about other's feelings although this can change in stressful or unfavorable environments. Your preferred style of motivation is persuasion, explaining the reasons behind the action, and leading by example in word and deed.

You clearly experience internal conflict, much more than most other profiles. While your primary dimension focuses on people, you may shift quickly to a focus on task and results. Your High I dimension is all about people, impulsiveness, risk, and the future. Your High C is about things, certainty, compliance, and status quo. You sometimes cannot see the trees for the forest, and other times cannot see the forest for the trees. You can be a risk-taker, or someone trapped in caution. You can be unplanned preferring to *wing it,* or you may be strongly organized and almost overly prepared. You may be the life of the party one minute and wanting nothing to do with people the next. You may be a big-picture dreamer in one setting and married to rules and policies in another. Fluctuating between these two conflicting dimensions may appear smooth and seamless, or it may appear quite abrupt at times.

You often act neither as a pure I nor pure C due to the thorough blending of the two dimensions (and the two below the line) creating a profile that is unique in itself. Your primary dimension focuses on people while your secondary focuses on tasks. However, you may bring both dimensions to bear in the same instance. Perhaps the simplest way this blending of the two dimensions manifests is with your conversations. You enjoy engaging with people but want the conversation to have substance and value where you both grow from it. In fact, sometimes you can lose track of time in a discussion, unaware that the other person would like to bring it to a conclusion. You also tend to think out loud because you value the dynamic of working through challenges with others. While collaboration can be powerful, it can lead to long debates that go in circles and seemingly never arrive at a clear conclusion.

A professor I worked with for many years loved the stage. The more people in the audience, the better. He not only was a great presenter in these large groups but also had the ability to work the audience with what appeared to be a natural flow, spinning easily from one audience member's comments to the next. What only a few of us knew was that public speaking terrified him. To mitigate his fears, he planned and prepared more than anyone I ever knew. He even prepared specific phrases just in case an audience member asked a very specific question in a very specific manner. And not only would he study and prepare, he would also practice saying certain things in different ways in the mirror. You can begin to see how conflicted the I/C profile can be, but also how beautifully the savvy I/C can blend those two dimensions into a single, extremely effective profile.

As you mature and learn to flow smoothly between the conflicting I and C dimensions, you display confidence and charisma balanced with fairness and critical thinking. You tend to be a strong communicator—your high C choosing your words prudently and your high I naturally gifted at influencing others. Your capacity to value both compassion and results serves you well in leadership positions, supporting your people but also holding them accountable.

Please read both the High I (Quadrant 2) and High C (Quadrant 4) narratives in the beginning of this chapter. See if some of the strengths and growth areas of both profiles resonate with you and then consider the applicable suggestions for growth offered in the *Moving Forward* narratives.

The

S/D

Quadrant 15

The S/D profile represents S and D dimensions above the line with I and C below the line. We all are a blend of all four dimensions, but the S/D profile behaves primarily with S tendencies and secondarily with D tendencies. This profile is so rare, many instruments do not even address it. It is estimated that only one-half of one percent of the population has the D/S or S/D profile.

Your primary dimension focuses on people while your secondary focuses on tasks. Taken together, you tend to be realistic and objective in your outlook but also conscientious in your approach. You place a high value on productivity. You may even judge yourself (and others) at the end of the day based on how much you accomplished. You also value how you accomplish the goal.

You try hard to be considerate of others and not hurt feelings, but in stressful times, you will resort to a more authoritative and domineering approach. Because you are people-oriented, you are inclined to take time for people even when you do not have that time to give. As a result, particularly with pressing deadlines and unfinished work, people can actually frustrate you when you perceive their presence as an obstacle to accomplishing your set goal.

You enjoy tough challenges but like to have your own space to deal with them—a space where you set your own timelines, pace, and approach to the extent possible. You do not respond well to others looking over your shoulders, hurrying you, and setting what you perceive as unrealistic time frames. You listen to people and sincerely value their interest and advice, but you tend to go through life with trial and error as your guide. Sometimes it takes two or three failures using the same behavior in the same context for you to alter your course. Your High S values transparency and relationships while your D values straightforward communication. People respect your fairness and sincerity as well as your strong determination and willpower.

Even with D as your secondary dimension, you still can lack self-confidence from time to time. Coupled with a strong sense of consciousness, often you will not delegate responsibilities because you do not want to overburden those around you, or simply because you know things will get done if you do it yourself. From time to time, you may be a little slow to get out of your comfort zone and start new things, but once you do, you never turn back. You are determined, persistent, and unflappable. Savvy S/Ds are very adept at giving others credit for a job well done while taking the blame when things do not go well.

Although you are adept at problem-solving and critical thinking, you rarely like to get wrapped up in details. If necessary, you can force yourself into the weeds of an issue, but details and minutiae frustrate you. You sometimes view specifics and preparation as obstacles that only slow you down from your goals. You appreciate structure and routine, but you easily become demoralized in a restrictive environment where you do not have a sense of control.

You experience internal conflict more than most profiles. Your High D is about power and control, more about results than people. Your High S is about warmth and teamwork, more about people than results. Your High S is patient, while your

High D is impulsive. Your High S wants peace and harmony, while your High D thrives in conflict and confrontation. Fluctuating between the two dimensions may appear smooth and seamless, or it may appear quite abrupt at times. You may be yelling one minute and apologizing the next. You can be the domineering leader in one context and the consummate follower in the next. One moment you are sitting in the back of the room somewhat shy and reserved and in the next moment barking orders in full command of the situation.

As you mature and learn to flow smoothly between the conflicting S and D dimensions, you display fairness, loyalty, and sincerity for those around you balanced with strength, confidence, and power. Your capacity to value both compassion and results serves you well in leadership positions. supporting your people yet also holding them accountable.

Please read both the High S (Quadrant 3) and High D (Quadrant 1) narratives in the beginning of this chapter. See if some of the strengths and growth areas of both profiles resonate with you, and then consider the applicable suggestions for growth offered in the *Moving Forward* narratives.

The

C/I

Quadrant 16

The C/I profile represents C and I dimensions above the line with D and S below the line. We all are a blend of all four dimensions, but the I/C profile behaves primarily with I tendencies and secondarily with C tendencies. This profile is rare. Indeed, many instruments do not even address it. It is estimated that only three percent of the population has the I/C or C/I profile.

DISC is predicated on perception—how you perceive your environment (favorable or unfavorable) and how you perceive yourself in relation to that environment (less powerful or more powerful). We will talk much more about this dynamic later in the text. Your C dimension emerges when you perceive your environment as unfavorable. You become withdrawn, impatient, even critical and will focus on task over people. When you perceive your environment as favorable, your I dimension tends to take over. When you are happy and want to be where you are doing what you want, you are friendly, outgoing, even charismatic, rallying people to your cause.

You often act neither as a pure C nor pure I due to the thorough blending of the two dimensions (and the two below the line), creating a profile that is unique in itself. Your primary dimension focuses on task while your secondary focuses on people. However, you may bring both dimensions to bear in the same instance. For instance, you like to blend creativity (High I dimension) with pragmatism (High C dimension). You are adept at combining intuition, logic, and critical thinking with strong people skills. Your preferred tools of motivation represent a blend of both dimensions as well—persuading, explaining the reasons behind the decision or task, and leading by example in word and deed.

Perhaps the simplest way the blending of the two dimensions manifests is with your conversations. You can be very direct but generally avoid harsh dialogue because you care about other's feelings, although this can change in stressful or unfavorable environments. You enjoy engaging with people but want the conversation to have substance and value, one where you both grow from it. In fact, sometimes you can lose track of time in a discussion, unaware that the other person would like to bring it to a conclusion. While collaboration can be powerful, it can lead to long debates that go in circles and seemingly never arrive at a clear conclusion.

You may be hypersensitive to scrutiny because of the extraordinary effort and precision you put into everything you do, coupled with your need (even if not self-evident) for social approval. You believe accuracy and details matter, but you also value the needs and feelings of those around you. At your worst, you may be viewed as self-righteous and self-absorbed. At your best, you have the capacity to be a person of significant power and influence.

You experience internal conflict more than most other profiles. While your primary dimension focuses on results, you may shift quickly to a focus on people. Your High C is about tasks, caution, compliance, and status quo. Your High I dimension is about people, impulsiveness, risk, and the future.

Your perception of environment and self also affect your external lens. You sometimes cannot see the trees for the forest, and other times cannot see the forest for the trees. You can be buried in caution and over-analysis or adept at risk-taking and spontaneity. You can be strongly deliberate and organized or unplanned and unprepared, preferring to wing it with your charm and gift of gab. You may be the life of the party one minute and want nothing to do with people the next. You may be married to rules and policies in one setting and a big-picture dreamer in another. Fluctuating between these two conflicting dimensions may appear smooth and seamless, or it may appear quite abrupt at times.

As you mature and learn to flow smoothly between the conflicting I and C dimensions, you display fairness and critical thinking balanced with confidence and optimism. You display strong communication skills—your High I dimension naturally gifted at influencing others and your High C dimension choosing your words prudently. Your capacity to value both results and compassion serves you well in leadership positions—supporting your people but also holding them accountable.

Please read both the High C (Quadrant 4) and High I (Quadrant 2) narratives in the beginning of this chapter. See if some of the strengths and growth areas of both profiles resonate with you and then consider the applicable suggestions for growth offered in the *Moving Forward* narratives.

The Tight Profile

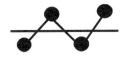

Quadrant 17

The Tight profile (sometimes referred to as a flat, neutral, or compressed pattern) shows all four dimensions very close to the horizontal line. It's a rare profile, representing approximately one percent of the population. While the pattern indicates you reflect all four dimensions with relatively equal value, it's possible that your responses on the assessment don't accurately reflect your true perceptions. The tight profile indicates self-contradictory responses, so much so they combine to cancel each other out.

I recommend taking the assessment again with a clearer focus, a clearer context in mind. Ask yourself if perhaps you were over-analyzing the questions by taking too long to respond; if so, focus this time on using your first choices. Finally, ask yourself if you really understood the meaning of each of the words and the correct process to complete the assessment.

If the pattern remains unchanged after retaking the assessment, it may indicate stress or discomfort in your life such as a significant emotional event, personal trauma, or unusually stressful external environment. More likely, the tight pattern probably indicates a profile devoid of extremes. You do not enjoy the strengths of the four dimensions to the extent as do other profiles, but you do not suffer the growth areas found in all four dimensions to the same extent either.

For the most part, you are even-tempered, steady, and adaptable to most situations. Yet, your behavior may still strongly represent any of the four dimensions, completely based on your perceptions.

More than any other profile, you flow among all four

dimensions equally throughout the day, depending on how you view your setting and yourself in relation to that setting. When you view your environment as unfavorable and yourself as more powerful, you behave in a manner consistent with the High D dimension—power, control, and confidence. When you view your environment as favorable and yourself as more powerful, you behave in the High I dimensions—outgoing, talkative, and persuasive. When you view your environment as favorable and yourself as less powerful than the environment, you behave in the S dimensions—sincere, supportive, and steady. When you view your environment as unfavorable and yourself as less powerful, you behave in the C dimension—cautious, compliant, and critical.

Please read all four narratives (D, I, S, and C) in the beginning of this chapter. I imagine you will find parts of you in all four. Do what you can to pull from the applicable strengths and weaknesses of all four profiles and consider the applicable suggestions for growth offered in the *Moving Forward* narratives.

THE FOUR DIMENSIONS OF DISC **6**

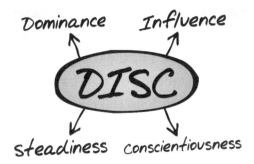

Dr. Marston, the creator of the DISC model, worked at a time when most of the research in human behavior involved the functions of mentally unhealthy minds. However, he was particularly interested in how normal or typical people behaved. He wanted to know what happened cognitively, emotionally, and physically when a person interacts with the world.

Marston measured respiration rate and galvanic skin response, leading to his role in developing the prototype of today's polygraph. His research included qualitative interviews, attempting to look deeper into human behavior. Marston identified categories of behavior present in all people but to varying degrees. In his 1928 publication, *Emotions of Normal People*, Marston divided human behavior into four distinct macro dimensions: D—Dominant or Directing, I—Inspiring or Interacting, S—Steady or Supporting, and C—Cautious or Compliant, none of which is better or worse than any other. Keep in mind, only about 5% of the population have just one dimension above the line. Most of us have two above and two below. Our response to the world is a nuanced product of where all four dimensions fall. It follows that not many of us will completely identify with all the descriptors offered in these pages.

It is worth mentioning again: Marston's identification of the four DISC dimensions was *not* an attempt to explain *why* people behave as they do. The *why* is incredibly complex and nuanced and deals with the entirety of one's personality (e.g., innate traits, learned characteristics, values, beliefs, character, and integrity, work ethic, life experiences, maturity), not just the observable or surface behavior described by the DISC model.

After having completed the assessment, you now have a very good understanding of your DISC dimensions. This is a good point in the text to begin exploring all four of the umbrella dimensions.

> In 15th century Europe, two men and two women are convicted of being witches. The special justice orders them to be burned at the stake. On execution day, all four are tied around a large post centered amid an impending blaze. With the entire town watching, the order is given to light the fire. The high executioner lights the brush only for it to immediately go out. He lights it again, and again it goes out. Five times he lights the fire, five times the fire goes out
>
> Believing this is divine intervention proving the accused witches' innocence, the justice orders all four of them released.
>
> The Dominant accused turns to the entire town and yells, "You see! I told you I was innocent!"
>
> The social Influencer shouts, "My friends, let's eat, drink, and party the night away!"
>
> The Steady and supportive accused walks up to the executioner and says, "I want you to know I do not hold this against you. I'm sure you are a

good person. You were just doing your job."

Finally, the Compliant, conscientious, critical thinker kneels to inspect the brush and the arrangement of the logs around the post. Turning to the crowd, he offers, "Hey, I think I see the problem."

D—Dominance

High D profiles may be described as demanding, assertive, decisive, competitive, self-assured, and willing to take risks. D profiles are motivated by challenge, change, action, and power. They thrive on autonomy and are easily demoralized in a restrictive environment. D profiles are generally less concerned with people and relationships, rather being focused on results and mission. They are competitive and want to win. As Vince Lombardi offered, "Winning isn't everything; it's the only thing."

Your focus on results sometimes may lead to a perception of High Ds as insensitive and pushy. High D profiles can become frustrated, even belligerent when they perceive others trying to take advantage of them or others. Their natural fight or flight response in a stressful situation is to fight.

Here's a High D scenario:

A husband and wife go the pharmacy to pick up a prescription. The pharmacy was extremely busy. After waiting 10 minutes in line, the following conversation occurred:

Pharmacist: I'm sorry, we don't have that medication in stock. However, I see in the computer that our store just 20 minutes from here does have it.

Wife: Thank you very much for checking. We will head that way.

Pharmacist: You are more than welcome. Have a great evening.

Husband: Ma'am, just a second. Please call that store and have the prescription waiting for us. That would save us at least 20 minutes this evening. I appreciate you doing this.

The wife was appreciative of the pharmacist's help and friendly attitude. It never even occurred to her to push on the pharmacist for more assistance.

However, the High D husband was mission-driven and despised wasted time. He had no issues whatsoever pushing the pharmacist, even though some would argue his behavior was a little rude and even selfish. After all, the pharmacist was swamped with her own customers and prescriptions to fill.

All four dimensions have powerful strengths, and all four have drawbacks as well. Please read the High D profile (Quadrant 1) in Chapter 4 for a fuller description of a profile with D above the line and the other dimensions below the line.

I—INFLUENCE

High I profiles are confident, expressive, optimistic, and popular. They will volunteer to lead and spend whatever amount of time necessary to develop buy-in to their ideas. They are motivated by prestige, recognition, and social approval, and they welcome opportunities to verbalize ideas and inspire others.

High C: I had a great weekend alone watching movies at home.

High I: Wow, really? Is that contagious? What can I do to make sure that never happens to me?

Those who are High I may have difficulty with time management and organization because of their propensity towards people as opposed to tasks. They fear social rejection and thrive on positive recognition. They can be fun people to have around because of their outgoing, often magnetic personality and playful side. However, they sometimes have difficulty knowing the difference between play time and game time or when to talk as opposed to letting others have the stage. The High I profile, above all else, is about engagement.

High I scenario:

Your High I profile son, Daniel, did not read a required book that was assigned two weeks ago for an oral presentation. This is typical for him because his charm, wit, and gift of gab usually carry the day. He did not even remember the assignment until he walked into class five minutes early to socialize and found everyone was stressfully reading and writing.

Daniel: Ally, what's everyone doing? It's so quiet in here.

Ally: Daniel, today is the big day that we give our oral presentations on those monster books we had to read. Everyone is freaking. I even read two books just in case.

Daniel: Ok, what's the name and author of your back-up book? In one sentence, what is the overall theme? And tell me one little part that really made you laugh or touched you in some way.

Ally answered the questions in two minutes. The teacher walked in, greeting everyone with a smile. She immediately called on Daniel, almost as if she knew he had not completed the assignment.

Daniel turned to Ally, winked his eye, and whispered with a smile, "You're going to love this." He confidently strode to the front of the class and thanked the teacher for the extremely valuable assignment and the opportunity to go first. He crushed the presentation, albeit short. He was funny, even a bit charismatic in his delivery.

But it wasn't over. The teacher asked, "Daniel, before you sit down, was there any one part of the book that particularly stood out to you—some specific anecdote perhaps?"

After a fictitious five seconds of deliberation, Daniel responded, "There absolutely was." He then went on to tell the class the fun little quip he had asked Ally to tell him before class.

It is easy to see the pros of the High I profile—confident, quick thinking, the great communicator. But it is similarly easy to see growth areas with some High I profiles—manipulative, deceptive, and lacking in substance because of their habitual reliance on their force of personality to win and succeed in life.

Please read the High I profile (Quadrant 2) in Chapter 4 for a fuller description of a person with I above the line and the other three dimensions below the line.

S—STEADINESS

High S profiles are loyal, dependable, balanced, considerate, and calm. They are great neighbors down the street or down the hall at work, and they always stand ready to help those they regard as friends. They may appear shy and even submissive but do not back them in a corner and expect no repercussions. They want peace and harmony but are not afraid to stand their ground, particularly in instances where they are protecting a friend or something that provides a sense of security. Because they are content people, they may be slow to change and too accepting of the status quo. Above all, High S profiles are team players concerned with harmony, cooperation, trust, and relationships.

High S scenario:

Four professors just received their end-of-the-course student evaluations. All four did well although plenty of growth areas were mentioned:

High D: I worked my butt off for them and gave it my best. Look at this—this person said I was the best instructor he ever had, yet he gave me a four out of a possible five. What is wrong with people!

High I: Wow, I am amazed I didn't do better. I was educational and super entertaining. And man, I thought I really connected with the class. Maybe they didn't like my stories or that I got a little off topic sometimes. I will work on all that for the next class.

High C: I followed the curriculum precisely, and this class scored higher on the same exams than the other professors' classes. They received an outstanding product from me. Some people just can't be pleased.

High S: I was expecting this. I had some good days but some bad ones too. They deserved 100% from me every class, and they did not get that. I wish there was some way to make it up to them. I guess all I can do is make things better for the next class.

You can sense from this short scenario the humility and sincerity found in the High S dimension. You can see how hard the High S professor took the bad surveys compared with the other profiles. High S profiles also often avoid conflict with others and even within themselves. They care about people and need people to care about them.

Please read the High S profile (Quadrant 3) in Chapter 4 for a fuller description of a profile with S above the line and the other three dimensions below the line.

C—COMPLIANCE

High C profiles are about compliance—compliance to rules, norms, practices, manners, and expectations. They are motivated by quality, accuracy, and consistency. High Cs also can be rigid and very critical of themselves and others. This may appear to others as them being somewhat aloof and even unapproachable, even if that is not the case at all. They are often loners preferring solitude to the company of others. High C profiles are detail-oriented, precise, cautious, and prepared. Sometimes this may lead to stagnation or over-analysis from being too bogged down in the details of a project or conversation. Here is a fun, albeit over the top, example of High C behavior.

High D: Hey, what time is it?

High C: It depends on the time zone, but I will cautiously assume you mean here. According to my watch, it is 10:14 am, but you should know my watch may not be exact. I can google the precise time on the World Clock if you prefer.

High D: I just asked you to tell me the time, not to build the freaking clock.

This exchange would be unusual even for a High C profile, but we do see this type of behavior frequently on a smaller level. For instance, I ask my wife what tomorrow's weather will be. All I am asking if for a couple of words—maybe temperature and rain or not. But in her desire to be correct and thorough, I can expect a detailed response to my question well beyond my wants and needs. However, with both of us understanding DISC, all I have to say is "clock-building," and she stops and grins.

I also have a responsibility to meet her in her comfort zone. I might listen to her details about the weather tomorrow without interruption and thank her afterward.

Let me offer an encounter I had a few years ago at work. A High C friend walked into my office at the FBI Academy with both hands cupped. He obviously had something precious and valuable in his hands.

"Hey, Jeff, where is your C-trash?" [*He was looking for the confidential trash bag most of us have in our offices for trash that's sensitive in nature for a variety of reasons. This trash would be shredded or burned per policy.*]

"It's behind my desk."

"Okay." He walked behind my desk and sprinkled what looked like a few crumbs into my C-bag, then abruptly walked out of my office with his hands still cupped with the remaining contents under close guard. He was on a mission of grave importance!

As he started out of my office and down the hall, I yelled, "Hey, hold up. What are you doing?"

"Jeff, it's that time of the year where we get new credit cards. I shredded my old one twice, and now I am going to distribute the crumbs equally in three different C-bags around the Academy."

I can hear the High D, I, and even S profiles laughing (or crying) right now. But this is perfectly logical and appropriate behavior for High C profiles. They are about precision, compliance, and getting things done perfectly the first time. They like to approach life according to plan—on time, on budget, always striving for excellence. This approach assists in their quest to be prepared for unforeseeable consequences and to even avoid altogether finding themselves in uncertain situations. It may be helpful to read the High C narrative (Quadrant 4) in Chapter 4 for a more in-depth look at that profile.

As with all profiles, strengths and growth areas always exist. We all look at the world differently and thus respond differently to it. This is a good thing. As the saying goes, it takes all kinds to make the world go 'round.

Perception is the key to understanding how people act and respond to the world around them. Dr. Marston, through his extensive research in the early 20th century, found that people act in accordance with how they perceive their environment (favorable or unfavorable) and their role in relation to that specific environment (less powerful or more powerful). It is important to understand moving forward that we do not view our environment and self in a particular way based on whether we are a D, I, S, or C. Rather, we behave as a D, I, S, or C because of how we perceive our environment and self.

This is not idle semantics. *Perception drives behavior, not the other way around.* Delving further into what drives perception (e.g., personality, motives, mood) is a great discussion but beyond the scope of this text and the DISC model.

The realization that perception drives behavior allows us to change our behavior to better meet the demands of the situation simply by changing the way we view the setting and ourselves. As you can gather from the following figure, people behave in the corresponding dimension relative to their perceptions.

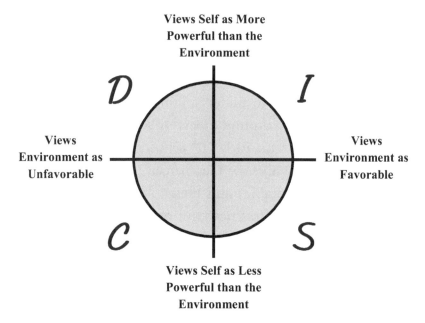

Perhaps an easier way to illustrate this concept is to call out each dimension individually.

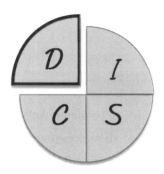

Environment is
perceived as
unfavorable /
Self is
perceived as
more powerful

Environment is
perceived as
favorable /
Self is
perceived as
more powerful

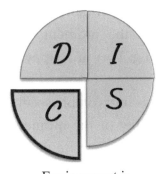

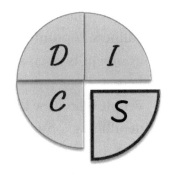

Environment is
perceived as
unfavorable /
Self is
perceived as
less powerful

Environment
is perceived
as favorable /
Self is
perceived as
less powerful

ENVIRONMENT: FAVORABLE OR UNFAVORABLE

Environment, in the context of the DISC model, simply means *everything beyond self*. Environment represents all the external influences impacting us throughout the day outside of the internal influences we bring to bear. Context is dynamic and fluid, often shifting not just throughout the day but often within minutes or even seconds. Thus, our perceptions of our environment are regularly fluctuating. We either view our environment as favorable or unfavorable.

People who view their environment as favorable see the friendliness, optimism, and warmth of the moment. The environment is open and non-threatening. They are happy to be there.

People who view their environment as unfavorable see the unfriendliness, obstacles, and even hostility of the moment. They are not happy to be there. Keep in mind, we are talking about perceptions, not necessarily reality. The environment could be friendly but perceived as unfriendly and vice versa. *Perception* is the key.

* * * *

Two coworkers are traveling out of town together on business. The first evening out, they get in their rental car and start driving around looking for a place to have dinner. They simultaneously spot a steakhouse on the left with a packed parking lot.

Mark: Hey, man, look at the parking lot. This place must be incredible to have that many people here. Let's go in.

Sean: What I see is us waiting in line all night. No way are we going there.

Both Mark and Sean see the exact same environment, yet each perceives it in a very different way. Mark perceives the environment through the lens of the S or I dimension while Sean views the environment through the lens of the C or D dimensions.

* * * *

Dad gets home from work about 6:30 after a long day. Mom got home from work minutes before and had just started dinner. Both were tired but in good moods. As the dad jumps in to help with dinner, they have this conversation:

Dad: Hey, sweetheart, how was your day?

Mom: Great, how about yours?

Dad: Great day, life is good—so anything on the agenda tonight? I'm really looking forward to a little rest and relaxation after dinner.

Mom: No rest for the weary tonight. Tommy has his parent/ teacher open house at school this evening, and Tammy has her ballet recital that she's in for the next three nights. I can't believe you forgot all of this. Looks like we are going in different directions tonight because they're both at the same time. Do you have a preference?

Dad: No preference at all; this just sucks. All right, let's eat and you choose.

Mom: You need to change your attitude. You get to spend quality time like this with your children. You'll miss this one day. Don't you know how lucky you are?

Both parents started dinner in a great mood—their environment was friendly, the future was bright, and life was good. But as perceptions often do, dad's perception of the environment quickly flipped to unfavorable. Mom's perception did not change.

The scenario highlights several key concepts of the DISC model. First, based on dad's unfavorable perception, he would then behave in either the D or C dimension dependent on how he saw himself in relation to the unfavorable environment. We saw that with his words "this just sucks" and his accompanying attitude. We also saw mom's behavior, which one of warmth and optimism—High I or High S.

Second, the situation was the same for both parents, yet they perceived it very differently. *Perception drives behavior.* Finally, we can alter our perceptions of the environment, thus changing our behavior. If dad can accept his wife's positive insights and perspective, his perception of the environment would immediately change, thus changing his entire behavior that evening. DISC describes how we typically react to our world, but it does not imprison us. We each have the power to choose how we behave.

SELF: MORE POWERFUL OR LESS POWERFUL

Power in this context means how much control or impact you believe you have on your situation. Those who view themselves as more powerful will behave in either the D or I dimension. They believe they can control the people and events around them either through dominance or persuasion. Those who view themselves as less powerful will behave in either the S or C dimensions. They believe they can have a greater impact on their environment by cooperating and following the rules.

Sometimes when I start explaining this concept, the High S and C profiles will raise their hands or, more often, not say anything during class but head straight to me during break. "I don't know what you mean by feeling less powerful. I don't feel less powerful than my environment."

Even after my humble attempts at explanation, I still seem to offend people sometimes with this assertion. Neither of the two perceptions (more powerful or less powerful) is more correct or appropriate than the other; they are just different just as we are all different. Consider, for example, two team members in a group meeting. The High I (views self as more powerful than environment) believes his role is to energize the group demonstrating passion and enthusiasm for the initiative. The High C (views self as less powerful than environment) believes his role is to provide details and facts of the initiative that would highlight its value. Both team members are committed to progress and accomplishment, simply in different ways.

Self-perception of power and control is a very complicated and nuanced concept and manifests in countless ways. Let's look at a few examples. We will start with an easy one most easily associated with feeling less or more powerful than one's environment.

* * * *

Two guys go out for a beer Saturday night while their wives are at an event in the neighborhood. They leave the bar around midnight. As they walk towards the car, several young men start to rapidly approach them from the dark alley.

Tom: Jimmy, we need to get to the car fast! Things are going south here quickly.

Jimmy: No, I think we'll slow down and handle things a little differently.

Again, no value judgments here. Both positions have their pros and cons. Tom feels less powerful than his environment while Jimmy certainly feels more powerful. Okay, that was an easy example of power in relation to environment. Let's make it a little more complicated.

On the way to a breakfast at the local restaurant, two friends go through the drive-through at Dunkin Donuts to get coffee. After arriving at the restaurant, Alison grabs her coffee and starts to get out of the car.

Kailey: Alison, you can't take that coffee in the restaurant.

Alison: Of course, I can.

Kailey: No, I'm serious. It's not allowed. They will ask you to leave.

Alison: You're crazy, I'm taking in my coffee.

Kailey: Either they're going to make you throw it away, take it back to the car, or you can cause a big scene with the manager. I don't want to be a part of any of that.

Alison: Relax, I'm not telling you to take your coffee. But I am taking mine.

Alison and Kailey walk inside and are immediately greeted with a big smile and warm welcome. Not one word about the large Dunkin Donuts coffee.

Kailey: Okay, Alison, wait until the waitress gets here. She's not going to like this.

Alison: Again, it's no big deal to them. And if it is, I'll just be nice while displaying strength and confidence. I guarantee no one will say a word.

The waitress was as warm and welcoming as the hostess had been.

Waitress: Can I start you ladies off this morning with coffee?

Kailey: No thank you, I'll have water.

Alison: No thank you, as you can see, I brought coffee.

Waitress: Sounds great. I'll be right back with your waters and to take your order.

Kailey and Alison were experiencing the same environment with the same people and events. Yet, they perceived it all very differently. Kailey wanted to be compliant with the rules and social expectations. She was fearful that Alison bringing in the coffee would cause drama and conflict, and they would be asked to leave. This is a classic case of feeling less powerful than your environment, which manifested in her C and S behaviors.

On the other side, Alison had no intention of causing problems, but she also had no intention of leaving her favorite coffee in the car to get cold. Alison owned the situation. She was confident and self-empowered. She perceived herself as more powerful than the environment, which led to her D and I behaviors.

Let's consider one more increasingly nuanced scenario surrounding power and self.

* * * *

The wife had been out of work for the past seven weeks because their family had recently moved. She made very good money in her line of work and was highly marketable. The husband also made good money, and they had a strong savings account for rainy days. The wife had two robust job offers an hour from home and two additional strong opportunities potentially on the horizon just five minutes from home.

Wife: I'm going to call those two companies an hour from here who have been courting me for the past couple of months.

Husband: What? You want to be on the road two hours a day when you could work here with a five-minute commute?

Wife: Honey, it has been six weeks. I need to work to help pay bills. Our finances were not set up for me to stay home. Who knows if the local offers will ever come, and if they do, how long from now will that be?

Husband: Sweetheart, wait it out. We are okay on money. I feel good about it. This is worth the wait.

Both the husband and wife view the environment as unfavorable—she is out of work thus no income. This indicates they will behave with either D or C characteristics. However, they see themselves in relation to that situation in a different light. The wife is conscientious in that she is feeling a little guilty about not contributing to the family income. She is insecure, apprehensive, almost scared that a new job near home will not happen soon enough. This also is what it can look like to feel less powerful than your environment. Thus, her response is consistent with the C dimension.

The husband is confident, optimistic, and willing to take the risk. This is what it can look like to feel more powerful than your environment—the D dimension. The point is that perceptions of power can be very subtle but have a significant and direct impact on our lives.

ORIENTATION: TASK V. PEOPLE / OUTGOING V. RESERVED

We have discussed how perception drives behavior—perception of the environment and ourselves relative to that environment. A more complete explanation is that Perception drives Orientation first. We are either more task-oriented or people-oriented in our goals or what we value most. We also are either more outgoing or reserved in how we approach or actionize those values. Orientation then, in turn, drives actual Behavior.

Task-oriented people are all about getting the job done. People-oriented folks are much more concerned with feelings and the journey we all take together achieving the goal.

Outgoing people seem to have a sense of urgency in most aspects of their lives. Their pace is quicker and more aggressive as they move forward in whatever the endeavor. Reserved people tend to be more deliberate in their thought and deed, often due to critical analysis of the situation, compliance, and conscientiousness of others.

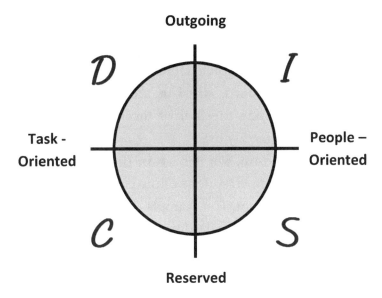

As depicted in the previous figure, the following profiles emerge, based on the person's orientation towards things or people, and their approach as either outgoing or reserved.

- Outgoing and task-oriented **D** Dimension
- Outgoing and people-oriented **I** Dimension
- Reserved and people-oriented **S** Dimension
- Reserved and task-oriented **C** Dimension

BEYOND THE FOUR DIMENSIONS: COMBINED/BLENDED PROFILES

As you noticed from the existence of 17 profiles discussed in Chapter 4 and the exploration of the theoretical underpinnings of the model in this chapter, DISC is not just represented by four categories. Indeed, *all* of us are a blend of *all* four dimensions—a mashing together of the behaviors we more readily use and less readily use.

In its simplest form, we behave in one dimension at a time informed by our perceptions of the environment and our role in that environment. For example, a person with an D/I profile primarily acts in the D dimension but secondarily in the I dimension. However, this may not tell the entire story. In other words, is the D/I profile someone who simply acts as an D sometimes and I sometimes, or does the mashing together of these two dimensions into one profile create something completely different—not quite D, not quite I?

Honestly, I am not sure. It could be the person flows so smoothly between the D and I dimensions that it looks like something unique but really is simply a frequent flow between the two dimensions. Indeed, Drea Zigarmi and colleagues hold that two dimensions cannot, at any single time, have equal importance under stress. Perhaps this is true in a crisis. Yet, I believe most of the time the thorough comingling of the two dimensions may actually create something unique altogether.

Little research exists in this specific area, so here is my view from years of exploration and observation. I believe in the simplicity of the DISC model—for the most part, a D/I is someone behaving sometimes as a D and less often as an I. But I also believe the mashing of the two dimensions does create something special and unique. Sometimes a story is the best illustrator of a point.

* * * *

From time to time, I have played pranks on people and had them played on me. One prank, in particular, demonstrates the notion of how a profile with two dimensions above the line actually may behave in a single instance not quite the top dimension and not quite the secondary but rather something unique in itself. I'll change the names of the players but not the facts of the prank.

This prank happened many years ago. I supervised two instructors in my unit who competed with each other in the classroom. Neither would admit it, but both were keenly interested in each other's student surveys. One competed in a more playful way, but the other with a more serious approach. In other words, it was not a big deal to one, other than to pick on the one to whom it was a big deal. This presented an opportunity for me to have a little fun.

I wrote a fictitious letter from the director of evaluations—a lofty position as there were hundreds of full time and collateral instructors—and addressed it to me as James' boss. The letter advised me that James (the instructor who was serious about the competition) was failing miserably in his student evaluations— evaluations that had yet to be released to James. I also provided several fictitious student quotes in the letter: *James is the worst instructor on the planet; James is the most arrogant and obnoxious instructor I have had in 32 years; James doesn't deserve to breathe the same air as the rest of us.*

And then one more for the kill: *I wish James was half the instructor that Joe is.* The last one was brutal. Joe was his competitor. The letter went on to say that the director had even pulled Joe's evaluations for comparison, and as indicated by the student quote, Joe was indeed one of the best instructors in the building. The letter even recommended I put Joe in for an award.

The letter concluded by directing me to get James more training on how to teach. If his evaluations did not go up signficantly with the next class, he would be terminated. I wrote a little note in the letter's margin and placed the letter in James' mailbox in the office. "James, please see me immediately about this letter." Of course, I let Joe and several others in on the prank.

A few hours later he walked to his mailbox, retrieved the letter and read it. He just stared at it, apparently reading it over and over. After a brutally long wait, I asked, "Hey, man, you okay? You look deep in thought."

"Yeah, yeah, it's just the letter you put in my box. I mean, boss, I'm sorry. I had no idea. I mean, I thought I was doing good. I, I just don't know . . ."

I said, as sincere and deadpan as I could pull off, "Well, hey, at least we have Joe." I thought James was going to lose it. As he was about to cry or yell, I wasn't sure which, I burst out laughing, as did Joe and a couple others who just happened to be passing by.

Some of you are laughing at my playfulness while some of you are incredulous at my lack of sensitivity. You both would be right. The High I in me informed the playfulness and manipulation. The High D informed the insensitivity (cruelty, you may say) and the confidence to even pull the prank in the first place. The prank was not quite I behavior nor quite D behavior. The behavior was the result of the thorough mashing together of I and D dimensions into something unique.

CLOSING THOUGHTS

Perception is the key to understanding how people act and respond to the world around them. The dynamic intersection of perception of

> *To change ourselves effectively, we first have to change our perceptions.*
> — Stephen Covey

self and environment forms the basis for the DISC model. It explains our orientations, which in turn explains our behavior. The model even offers the capacity to predict future behavior of self and others. The tremendous value of this foundation rests in the ability to change our behavior by changing our perceptions of the environment and self. As Dr. Wayne Dyer offered, "The more you change the way you look at the world, the more the world begins to change."

RECOGNIZING OTHERS
WITHOUT THE INSTRUMENT

As you become more familiar with the DISC model, you undoubtedly will start to recognize behaviors in yourself and others that correspond to the various dimensions. Eventually, you will get fairly adept at identifying a person's profile just in the time it takes for a handshake and greeting.

Getting to this point starts with deliberate observation of the nuances at that moment. Was the hand shake firm or gentle? Did she look me in the eyes? Did I sense sincerity or power? Did she carry the introduction, hardly allowing me to talk, or was she quiet, letting me do the talking? Did he speak in bullets or more in the narrative? What was his appearance: organized or disheveled? What was her physical demeanor: poised and firm or relaxed, maybe even slouching? Did she look me in the eyes, or did she glance elsewhere, even towards the floor? The nuances of the moment are endless.

In the beginning, it will take a lot of energy and effort to mentally address these distinctions while keeping your head in the conversation. But after a while, you will almost subconsciously ask and answer these questions, identifying their profile with little to no thought at all.

The most accurate way to assess someone's profile in the quickest amount of time may be to consider their orientation towards direct or indirect action and their orientation towards

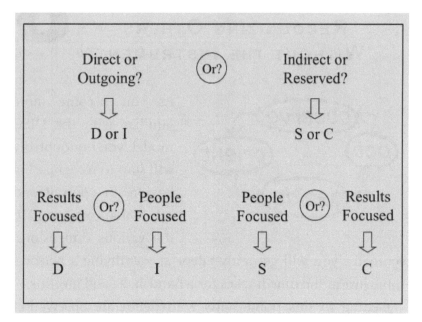

an outgoing or more reserved approach. From there, consider their orientation towards people or tasks.

Consider an interaction you have with a potential employer. She already has your résumé, but this is the first occasion you've talked. Your appointment is at 2:40 pm, not 2:30 or even 2:45. You arrive at 2:30 as to be respectfully early but not too early. The hiring manager walks out into the waiting area at 2:35, speaks briefly with her secretary, and then retreats to her office. You were impressed with her flawless outfit and poise.

At 2:40, the secretary escorts you to the manager's office. She politely thanks you for being prompt and then asks three specific questions related to your résumé. She remains expressionless while you give your responses. She abruptly ends the interview by welcoming you on board with the company.

There are plenty of clues as to the manager's DISC profile. First, considering the illustration above, look at her orientation towards being direct or indirect. In both word and action, she demonstrated a very direct demeanor. She was direct with her questions and clearly drove the conversation as well as how long the conversation lasted. Thus, we assess her as a D or I.

Then ask yourself if she was more about tasks and results or people. More clues abound. Look at the specificity of the time the interview was scheduled. She is not one to waste time. Look how she is dressed—absolutely impeccably. Finally, consider the conversation. No wasted idle small talk. No building of a rapport. No selling of the company. She is all about business, all about results. Looking at the previous illustration, we can assess her as a High D (with C probably as her secondary dimension).

Let's practice with a few quotes from famous people and movies. See if you can identify the highest dimension associated with each quote. Keep in mind, all we have is a quote. All we can say is that the quote displays a certain profile at that point in time. It would be too great of a leap to ascribe that profile to the author based on just one quote that we have out of context.

FILL IN THE BLANK WITH D, I, S, OR C

A man may dwell so long upon a thought that it may take him prisoner.

Lord Fairfax _____

No act of kindness, no matter how small, is ever wasted.

Aesop _____

You can't handle the truth!

A Few Good Men, 1992 _____

I've never been a sunny personality.
I've never been outgoing. I'm a solitary person.

Jessica Lange _____

I don't like to repeat successes. I like to move on to new things.

Walt Disney _____

Plan your day for today and every day, then work your plan.

Margaret Thatcher _____

An eye for an eye only makes the whole world blind.

Mahatma Gandhi _____

You know the difference between you and me?
I make this look good.

Men in Black, 1997 _____

This is no time for ease and comfort.
It is time to dare and endure.

Winston Churchill _____

When you're just like everybody else, you've nothing to offer other than your conformity.

Dr. Wayne Dyer _____

A calm and modest life brings more happiness than the pursuit of success combined with constant restlessness.

Albert Einstein _____

We've got some difficult days ahead. But it really doesn't matter with me now because I've been to the mountaintop . . .
I've looked over and I've seen the promised land. I may not get there with you. But I want you to know tonight that we as a people will get to the promised land.

Dr. Martin Luther King, Jr. _____

A census taker once tried to test me. I ate his liver with some fava beans and a nice Chianti.

The Silence of the Lambs, 1991 _____

First, the Lord Fairfax quote. What type of profile/person is he talking about? He is ostensibly complaining about someone who appears to be task-driven as opposed to people-driven since the person is all about some apparent project or decision. This puts the person in either the C or D dimension. The quote also describes a person consumed with details and perfection. As High Ds like to get it done and move on, the High C profile remains.

How about Aesop's profile as demonstrated by his quote? Any of the four dimensions can show kindness, so no way to know for sure. However, the focus on people indicates high S or I. And the omnipotence of kindness in the quote probably indicates a High S profile.

Who will ever forget Colonel Nathan Jessep's (Jack

Nicholson) response to Lt. Daniel Kaffee (Tom Cruise) in *A Few Good Men*: "You can't handle the truth!" The response exuded confidence and power. It was said with utter contempt and disdain for Lt. Kaffee and the entire process of questioning his leadership. Colonel Jessep showed fierce independence and a disregard for the rules as he thought his actions were in the best interest of the Corps and Country. Clearly this quote, and surrounding tone and context, demonstrate High D behavior.

Jessica Lange perfectly described a High C profile, reserved and solitary.

Walt Disney's quote is interesting. It shows hints of task and people. The need to move from one project to the other, one decision to the next, is D behavior. So too is his confidence and inclination to bore easily. Yet, the quote is inspirational and shows great optimism for the future. Walt Disney probably has both D and I above the line.

Plan and work the plan. Margaret Thatcher's remarks indicate a strong propensity towards organization, details, accuracy, and perseverance—all High C behavior.

Gandhi's quote is about forgiveness, generosity, and peace. It is not about weakness or submission. It is about compassion—classic High S behavior.

How about Will Smith in *Men in Black*? Confident, smooth… "I make this look good." High I behavior.

Churchill's quote shows unequivocal power, call for action, and risk-taking—High D behavior. But that last word, *endure*, is consistent with both D and C behavior. Ds want to win, failure is not an option, but Cs can be doggedly determined. The irony is that I can almost hear him saying this quote in his powerful yet persuasive and inspirational tone—High I behavior. Churchill may be one of the 15% who has three dimensions above the line.

Dr. Dyer's quote speaks to the power of individualism and negative effects of conformity—High D and High I behavior. Indeed, High S and C profiles desire the security of conformity and status quo.

Albert Einstein was clearly highlighting the value in a calm, humble, and sincere approach to life—all High S behavior.

Dr. King's inspirational quote is about a brighter future. The specific words and phrasing were eloquent and beautiful. The message was powerful and moving. He painted an inspirational picture for us of what is to become if we try hard enough—High I behavior.

Lastly, consider the words of Hannibal Lecter (played by Anthony Hopkins) in the *Silence of the Lambs*. Yep, trick question! In a time when most psychologists were interested in the mentally deranged, Dr. Marston created the DISC model towards the further study of normal or typical people. Assessing Hannibal Lecter's behavioral preferences is beyond the scope and design of the DISC model.

* * * *

Two coworkers (Katey and Justin) walk into the conference room at work to meet the new employee. The new employee appears somewhat aloof and indifferent. Katey extends her hand to greet him. "Very glad to have you on board with us. My name is Katey." The new employee forces a small smile and says nothing. He does not extend his hand. After a very awkward few seconds, Katey drops her hand and eases away.

As Katey quietly exits the conference room, Justin approaches the new employee, firmly gripping the man's shoulder. "Exactly what is your problem, not shaking Katey's hand?"

What was Katey's highest dimension? _____

Justin's? _____

The new employee's? _____

Katey exhibited strong High S behavior. She was friendly, supportive, and sincere. She introduced herself with warmth and appreciation for the new employee. When her handshake was rebuffed, she quietly accepted the situation and eased out of the room almost unnoticed.

Justin, however, was livid. The nerve of this new guy to be so disrespectful and standoffish towards someone who was just trying to be nice. Justin stayed calm but confronted the employee in a clear and direct manner. All High D behavior.

Guessing the new employee's profile is not as simple. After all, each of us can have a bad day. Or maybe the new employee is an acute germaphobe with social anxieties. Let's go back to the theory behind DISC for a little help.

It is fairly obvious he viewed his surroundings as unfavorable. That places him in either the D or C dimension. We then need to be able to ascertain if he feels more powerful or less powerful than his environment. We really have no way of knowing from this simple encounter. Let's try one more way of estimating his profile that we talked about in the beginning of this chapter. Was he direct and outgoing? Not at all. This places him in either the S or C dimension. Was he then more people-oriented or task-oriented? Clearly, he did not display an affection for people. This narrows him to the High C dimension.

* * * *

My wife and I were out to dinner. Six older women were sitting at the table beside us. As they were preparing to leave, the waiter walked over to the table, looked at each of them with sincerity and confidence and said, "Of all the places you could have dined this evening, you chose to spend your time with me. I am honored and very appreciative of that. Have a beautiful weekend, ladies." The women nearly melted into their seats.

After they left, my wife called the waiter over to our table. Smiling, she said, "That was amazing—totally smooth yet total BS." All three of us started laughing.

The waiter grinned, "Yeah, I'm very good at what I do, but that one tested me."

What was the waiter's highest dimension? _____

The waiter displayed High I tendencies. He was confident and people-oriented. What he lacked in sincerity (he played those ladies with the smoothness of a pro), he made up for in making the ladies feel special and important—they mattered.

* * * *

Four coworkers were looking for a local gym to exercise in during lunch or after work. They walked in together to Global Fitness a block from their work. As they waited for a tour, they stood together at the counter in silence but all making internal observations and judgments.

> "This place is super busy. Ugh, I don't have time to socialize at the gym. I want to power through my work out and get back to the office." _____

"This place is super busy. I will be the center of it all in no time with my personality!" _____

"This place is super busy. It's a little intimidating, but I'm so excited about working out with my new friends from work every day." _____

"This place is super busy. Where is the salesperson anyway? We need to get back to the office before our 60 minutes for lunch is up. I wonder how many hours this equipment can hold up under the constant pressure of all these people. How many paying clients do they have? Let's see, if they have __ clients and the expenses are__, they are making way too much money on us." _____

The gym was very busy, and they all perceived it as such. Yet, the similarities largely stopped there.

The first coworker was not pleased. When he goes to the gym, he does not want to be bothered by people. He likes the energy of the gym, and he likes being able to see others push themselves. In fact, the silent competition motivates him. But too many people there, especially socializing, was not a good thing—High D behavior.

The second coworker loved the busy nature of the gym. She loved the idea of so many people sharing a passion and vision for better health and growth. She saw opportunities not only socialize but to actually become the center of attention. It was a crowd, and she loved working crowds—High I behavior.

The third coworker liked the social aspect of so many people working out together, but the volume was a little overwhelming. He likes being around people but usually small groups of friends or family—High S behavior.

The fourth coworker largely ignored the high number of people. She's been developing coping mechanisms for that her entire life. What she really focused on were the details such as the life-cycle of the equipment, even doing the math in her head as to the fairness of the cost of membership—High C behavior.

* * * *

Their elderly mother was in an assisted living home suffering from dementia. The four children (ages 43, 45, 51, and 55) were doing their best to visit mom and take care of her needs while still trying to take care of their immediate families and work. The past few years had been very difficult, as you can imagine.

Aunt Terri (mom's sister) lived close but seldom visited. This morning after one of her rare visits, Aunt Terri texted all four of the children in a group chat. "I just left your mother's room, and she's out of shampoo. What is wrong with you? You always put yourself ahead of your mother's needs."

> "Aunt Terri, I get your frustrations with your sister's condition. I get your fears of the same thing happening to you, and you not having anyone to take care of you like we do our mother. But your comments were not well-received as they were both wrong and inconsiderate, considering the vast amount of time we do spend with mom. Words matter. Consider your words more carefully. Please feel free to call me if you like to discuss this more. I will stop by your house if you like." _____

"The nerve and absolute insanity of you thinking you know anything or have anything of value to contribute to us is astounding. This is the last time you ever chastise us for anything."   _____

"Terri, what is your email address? I am going to immediately send you my Excel spreadsheet detailing each of our visits, how long we stayed, and what tasks we accomplished. The facts clearly speak for themselves."   _____

"Aunt Terri, your remarks hurt my feelings. We all are trying so hard to manage work, home, and mom. We're not always perfect, but we love our mother and would do anything for her. I will be glad to pick you up and take you with me to visit mom more often, so you can get a better picture of how hard we are working and how much we really do care."   _____

The first quote was like the fourth quote in many ways. Both showed a level of tact. Both showed a willingness to engage and even talk further about the issue. There were subtle but powerful differences too. The first quote showed an annoyance with Aunt Terri's text, while the fourth quote showed how it hurt this person's feelings. The final difference is the most nuanced yet the most important.

The writer of the fourth quote wanted reconciliation. The writer of the first quote wanted to hurt Aunt Terri as demonstrated with the subtle jab about Aunt Terri's fears and having no one in her life that loves her. The first quote indicates High I behavior. The fourth quote demonstrates High S behavior. The second quote is clear. High D profiles attack and hold people accountable, sometimes with little tact or care for other's feelings. Finally, the third quote highlights details, accuracy, facts, and evidence…all High C behavior.

CLOSING THOUGHTS

With a little effort, energy, and observation skills, you will begin to identify the profiles of those you meet throughout the day. You will notice strong clues based on what they say and do, how they say and do it, even in the way they present themselves.

Quite often, of course, one or two clues is not enough. If you see a person melting down in anger, it would be intuitive perhaps, but nevertheless incorrect, to assume he is a High D. However, it could be his High C dimension is overwhelmed with too many tasks to get done in too short a time frame. Or maybe it is his High S dimension finally pushed to a breaking point with a coworker's constant condescending and rude remarks. Really all we know from seeing that angry man is that there is an angry man.

I also used to teach with an outstanding instructor who had a C/D profile. Yet, in the classroom, he was passionate, outgoing, even what most would consider to be charismatic— all High I profile characteristics even though his I dimension was extremely low. But as a seasoned educator, he knew most students resonated with this type of high-energy instruction. He had developed the ability to change his behavior and go beyond his comfort zone to fit the needs of the situation, which is the quintessential value of the DISC model.

Determining behavioral profiles is not always easy. Sometimes it requires more time to study verbal and non-verbal clues. Yet, with a little practice, it will not take long before you are very capable of making those assessments quickly and accurately.

NOW WHAT?
EFFECTIVE INTERACTION AMONG
THE DIMENSIONS

9

Henry Van Dyke offered, "In the progress of personality, first comes a declaration of independence, then a recognition of interdependence." Now that we have an understanding and appreciation of the DISC model's behavioral profiles, it's time to do something positive with this knowledge. We end the chapter with scenarios illustrating the value and actual use of the model. We begin with some fun, showing how different profiles view and respond to the world and each other.

Keep in mind, only about five percent of the population has the sole dimension of D, I, S, or C above the line on their graph with the other three below the line. Most of you have a secondary dimension above the line that may have just as much impact on your behavior as your primary dimension.

****

Four people are in a car traveling eastbound on a four-lane interstate (two lanes each direction with wooded median strip in the middle). The speed limit is 65 mph. Two cars are blocking the road in front of them—one in the right lane and one in the left lane. Both blocking cars are traveling 65 mph.

High D—Driving, of course. He starts riding the bumper of the car in the left lane, no more than three feet behind it, attempting to bully the car to speed up and move over to the right lane. The High D is getting more furious by the minute. "Why do we let freaking idiots drive on our highways? Get out of my way!"

High I—Her competitive and playful side is starting to show. She also wants to get by the car. Not because she is being taken advantage of, which is really what is bothering her High D friend, but because she wants to win this challenge. Her go-to tool is communication. "Hey, blow the horn or flick your high beam. If that doesn't work, wait for a space to blow by him, and I'll moon him as we go by."

High S—"Please slow down and just let it go. It's not worth dying over. The tension is making me very uncomfortable. You are going to ruin the entire evening."

High C—Also irritated and becoming unusually confrontational. "Yeah, he deserves this. Doesn't he know the law or at least the social expectation that slower drivers stay to the right and faster drivers stay to the left? But hey, you are driving too close. Three feet does not give us enough stopping time if he slams on his brakes. Remember the two-second rule when following vehicles."

* * * *

You arrive at the service department to pick up your car that was supposed to be ready at 10:00 am. It is now 4:00 pm, and the car is still not ready. You have rescheduled three client appointments this afternoon and have a 5:15 pm meeting with a new client. You explain this to the service representative who says they are doing the best they can. Four customers waiting in the lobby overhear your conversation.

High D—"Ma'am, a quick word with you. His excuse is utter BS! You were wronged, and his attitude makes it even worse. Either rip him alive right now or go straight to the general manager of the dealership. I'll do it for you if you like."

High I—He walks over to you immediately, smiling and extending his hand. "Hi, I'm Jimmy. Do you mind if I talk to the service rep and manager on your behalf? I'm sure I can get your car to you in no time and probably get you some coupons for your next service call, or maybe even some money off the cost of this visit?"

High S—Stays in her seat in the lobby, continuing to read her book. She says to herself, "This is none of my business and interfering will only cause drama I do not need in my life."

High C—"Ma'am, not my call, but you cannot let this go. You entered into a social contract with the dealership that your car would be repaired by 10:00 am. Their breach has negatively impacted your work, productivity, and possibly professional relationships. You need to immediately speak with the general manager and complete a detailed customer service survey to the corporate office in Detroit."

Did you notice pretty much the same response from the High D and High C in both scenarios? Their tone was a little different, but both craved accountability and action. The real difference in their response was not the behavior but the underlying motive. The D felt taken advantage of and wanted to cause pain to the accused. The C felt the driver in the first scenario and the service rep in the second scenario had broken the rules, and moreover, this defiance caused suffering.

This is a significant nuance in understanding the DISC Model. Sometimes behaviors will appear the same with different profiles. The difference is the motive. Let me offer one more illustration about this important point.

A few years ago, I participated in a two-week leadership course sponsored by a well-known and respected university. The first day of class, the instructor told us the hours would be 8:30 am to 5:00 pm with an hour-and-a-half lunch. However, if the class wanted to get out at 4:30 pm, we could vote to take only one hour for lunch.

The class consensus was unanimous—cut lunch short and leave early. We all rushed to the local food places and barely made it back on time. 4:30 pm came and went with the instructor in full stride. At 4:55 pm, he wrapped up his remarks and kind of apologized. "Thank you for staying past our agreed-upon time. I was making a very important point that I wanted to finish before we leave."

How do you think the class responded? Well, no one overtly mutinied, but the class was not amused. It would be easy to say, "Hey, what's the big deal. It's only 25 minutes." But it was more principle than substance to most. Each of the students displayed one consistent behavior: They all complained to the program coordinator early the next morning. This same behavior was displayed across all the four DISC profiles surely represented in the class.

How is it that all four DISC dimensions can act in the same way? It may be because they actionize that macro behavior in very different ways. However, sometimes it may be because motive is the only discernable difference. I don't want to get too wrapped up with motive. Right or wrong, action is really the measure most of us use with our judgements. As Stephen M. R. Covey offered, "We judge ourselves by our intentions; we judge others by their behavior." But motives can be important. Consider the motives here.

High D—What a liar. He's so lucky I try to be respectful in public. I'm going to let the program manager know first thing in the morning what happened. It's his responsibility to handle this. But I'm ripping this instructor's head off if I don't get the right response from the manager and him.

High I—He entered into a social agreement with us and broke it. I made plans to eat dinner out with my family this evening because of the deal we made this morning. Now, they are at the restaurant having fun and eating without me.

High S—I don't understand why he thinks *his* wants are greater than *ours*, why his interests outweigh the clear agreement we had, an agreement that was *his* idea in the first place. I'm not going to confront him because it won't matter, but I will talk to his boss tomorrow morning. His behavior was not considerate at all.

High C—He lied. No getting around it. We had a concrete deal that he willfully violated. He broke the rules and needs to be held accountable. This should never happen again and talking with his boss is the only way to ensure that.

High D's value control and power. The High D in this scenario demonstrated this need to fix the problem clearly and directly and rather forcefully if necessary. He also judged the motives of the instructor—a liar.

Very different from the High D, the High I student was motivated by people and social concerns. The High S student valued fairness and harmony. "Why does he think his wants are more important than ours?" The High C student was motivated by compliance. The instructor broke the rules and needed to be held accountable. All four profiles engaged in the same macro behavior but were motivated to do so in very different ways.

One more important element to highlight before moving on: We *all* behave in *all* four dimensions throughout the day. Those of us with dimensions very low on the graph may not often exhibit traits associated with those dimensions, but we do from time to time. For those of us with two above the line and two below the line, we fluctuate often between our primary and secondary dimensions.

Consider the scenario at the car dealership. The High S customer in the lobby decides to avoid conflict by not getting involved. But what if she had both S and C above the line (S/C profile). How might she respond? She may have behaved in the same way as described above because, after all, her highest dimension is S. However, she may have responded with her secondary C dimension, which is a completely different response.

Remember the theory informing the DISC model. How do we view the world, and how do we view ourselves in relation to the world? In this scenario, she acted with S tendencies. However, once her view of the setting starts becoming unfriendly, as it may if the conflict grows, she would switch to her C dimension

My point here is simple but significant. About 80% of us have two dimensions above the line. *The secondary dimension is just as important as the primary.* In fact, where the bottom two dimensions fall on your graph even plays a significant role in determining how you respond to your fluid and everchanging settings.

Do Birds of a Feather Flock Together?

When engaging in conversations about the interaction of the various dimensions with one another, I often get asked this simple but great question: Do birds of feather really flock together? It seems a lot of us want to know if we are attracted to those who are similar to us.

Or is it the other age-old question: Do opposites attract? I usually start that conversation by asking what their DISC profile is as well as that of their spouse or significant other and their best friend. Overwhelmingly, the profiles of the student and those closest to them by choice (you can't choose your kids or parents) are different, often completely different. The research is interesting in this field.

After a review of studies in the area of romantic relationships, Dr. Vinita Mehta concluded people are more likely to pursue romantic relationships with people who are more like themselves across a broad range of characteristics including age, religion, political alignment, and education.

Psychologist Matthew Montoya examined the combined results of over 200 studies in this area over the past 50 years. He found an irrefutable relationship between similarity and attraction. One review of over 300 research studies comprising

35,000 participants found similarity was a robust predictor of attraction. The review found no evidence that opposites attract.

Sarah Knapton, Science Editor for *The Telegraph,* offered, "The theory that opposites attract is a myth . . . . scientists have found that people are only attracted to those who hold the same views and values as themselves."

Professor Angela Bahns observed, "Selecting similar others as relationship partners is so widespread on so many dimensions that it could be described as a psychological default."

The evidence is clear that birds of a feather do tend to flock together. But let's revisit how I opened this topic. Consider your spouse or significant other. Do you share the same DISC profile? My guess is you do not. I bet many of you share very different profiles. And I bet most of you are in happy relationships, notwithstanding all relationships have their difficulties and stressors.

So, how can this be when most of the research points in the opposite direction? I think people are attracted to those who share similar core values, beliefs, work ethics, and morals. However, sharing our lives with people who respond to the world in the very same way we do can be boring and stifling. It is exciting and fulfilling to be around people with different personalities. I imagine each of us has some inner drive for completion in our lives.

As I reflect on my relationships throughout my life, I have surrounded myself, either consciously or not, with people who have very different personalities than me. My DISC profile is D/I. My best friend in college was a S/D. My best friend in the police academy and for many years after that was an S/C. My closest friend in my early days in the FBI was a C/S. My best friends today, outside of family, are a high D, C/S, and S/I. My wife's profile is S/C. I like to think of these relationships as complementary.

Where I lack, my wife is strong. Where she has room for growth, I excel. Even in our needs and behavioral preferences, we balance each other. She is understanding (mostly) for my need to be in control. We rarely fight over who holds the TV remote. I appreciate her need for stability and security. She handles the finances and bills, so she can visibly see every month that we're doing okay. I push on people. She supports people. I go through life at light speed. Her pace is more deliberative and paced. I push her out of her comfort zone while she grounds me. We balance each other.

Even though we complement one another's behavioral preferences, we still have conflict. Her incessantly kind approach drives me crazy at times as my more controlling approach often frustrates her. People call her an angel and me a bull in a china shop. She walks through the grocery store literally smiling at everyone. I want to get in and out of the grocery store with zero social interaction. Yet, we make it work. I am convinced our differences contribute to our strong relationship. Our individual differences form our combined strength.

The research is convincing that opposites do not attract, but that has not been my experience. Perhaps, it is not so much about similar or dissimilar personalities as much as it is about understanding our preferences and needs and sharing important, deep-rooted values. Family, service to others, honor, and faith are important to both my wife and me. We even share similar views on spending, fitness, and a variety of other characteristics important in a marriage.

Even when we express those values differently, we still hold them dearly in a macro way. Consider fitness for example. We are both in the gym nearly every day, even when traveling. I prefer to lift heavy with fewer reps while she prefers high reps and lower weight. I prefer anaerobic cardio, such as HIITs, while she prefers aerobic cardio on the treadmill, elliptical, or rower. We both place a high value on fitness and exercise, but we approach that value differently.

The most successful relationships are built on the appreciation of both the similarities and differences each person brings to the relationship. Maybe it is more about how we engage with one another, how we employ our behavioral preferences, as opposed to the preferences themselves.

Whether we are looking to improve our relationships with friends, family, clients, or coworkers, our ability to understand our own behavioral preferences and those of others has a welcome impact on the relationships.

IMPROVING COMMUNICATIONS WITH WHAT YOU NOW KNOW

The overarching benefit of the DISC model is self-awareness, which ostensibly leads to other-awareness. But this new knowledge is for naught if we do not act with it, if we do not change our behavior based on the needs of the situation. Behavioral flexibility and adaptability are the foundation of effective relationships. Successful people meet people in their comfort zone. They consider the other person's needs and personality. Why wouldn't we all want to do this? Why would anyone want to be a prisoner of their own behavioral preferences and profiles?

The most practical and easily actioned result of the model rests with better communication with others. Consider a simple disagreement between my wife and me. She is an S/C, and I am a D/I. In circumstances I perceive as unfavorable, I almost always display High D behavior—control, confrontation, even raising my voice if unchecked. However, this behavior shuts my wife down. While I seem to love conflict at times, my yelling or determination to win causes an invisible, yet powerful, wall to go up between us. As a result, I

> *Raise your adaptability and you'll discover trust and credibility go up; lower it, and they go down. Behavioral adaptability means adjusting your behavior to allow others to be more at ease, encouraged, and successful in your relationship.*
>
> —Tony Alessandra
> Michael O'Connor

become completely ineffective in my capacity to influence or change her mind.

However, if I consider her DISC profile before opening my mouth, my influence expands exponentially. She is a great listener. She is calm and sincere. If I adapt my approach to meet her steadiness and need for safety and security, I actually have a chance to finally win an argument. Even if I lose, I will not make matters worse.

I do not have to become an S/C to practice effective adaptability. I simply need to tone down my High D behavior to avoid intimidating or controlling her or creating a tense, stressful environment her High S dimension does not appreciate. I could change my attitude from one of win at all costs to one of seeking a win/win result. Maybe I could even ask questions and actually listen. And perhaps I make sure I have my position points well evidenced and articulated to meet her C dimension.

Each of us can practice flexibility and adaptability and

become good at it. None of the four DISC dimensions is better at this than the others. But it does take practice. It takes time, energy, effort, and commitment.

Consider the following scenario that demonstrates the practical value of the DISC model in the workplace—adaptive behaviors that lead not only to improved communications but also expanded influence and more effective leadership.

For a few years, I worked for a person with a High I profile. After his retirement, he was replaced by a High D profile. Both were great bosses and great people, yet they were very different in many ways. Given what we have discussed thus far about these two profiles, how should I communicate with them?

You may be asking, "What do you mean communicate differently with them? I communicate the same way with everyone." I would encourage you to fight that inclination. Sure, all of us want to be consistent and genuine in how we communicate, but we should meet people in *their* comfort zone, not *ours*.

Here is an example of how I often approached communicating with them to increase my influence and effectiveness.

If I had an idea for a new program or possible fix for some challenges we were having, I would go to their office, knock on the door, and talk with them. Yet, how I talked to them, even how I knocked on the door, was different. The first boss was a High I profile. He was all about people. He liked talking in the narrative and mixing business with pleasure. Relationships were more important to him than programs or things in general. He was optimistic and was energized by passion and enthusiasm in others.

Equipped with this understanding, I would go to his office, knock on the door in a fun way, and stick my head in with a big smile. He would welcome me in with open arms motioning me to sit in one of his comfortable chairs or the sofa. He would come around from his desk and join me around the coffee table. I would then spend several minutes asking him about the weekend, the family, just small talk, giving us a chance to catch up, particularly if we had not spoken in a while.

Then I would gradually move into my presentation, making sure he could sense, almost feel, my excitement about the idea. I would spend time about the journey ahead and how powerful this journey would be pulling the entire unit together working on a common, valuable project together. Providing my idea was sound, this approach seemed to work well.

After his retirement, the new boss came in—a High D profile. As you know by now, Ds often can have powerhouse personalities. My new boss was not the loud or yelling type, but he was always in control. He was clear and direct with his communications. Not one to waste time, he talked almost in bullets and expected the same in others. He admired people who were clear in their words and was more than mildly annoyed by what he perceived as smooth talkers. He was quick to make decisions, too.

I would go to his office and knock on the door with two strong blows. He would say, "Enter." I would then approach his desk, choosing to stand, primarily because this was not a social call, and secondly because there was no real place to sit other than a couple fold-up chairs. [When he got the job, he immediately removed the nice, comfortable furniture my previous boss had. To this day, I think he did that because he did not want anyone getting too comfortable and staying too long.] I would then say in bullet format, "Boss, you know we have had problems with ___; I have a fix that I'd like to discuss with you. I'll have a one-page executive summary to you by the end of the day. After you digest it, let me know if you're interested, and I'll set up a time to brief you." After a nod from him, I would leave.

Some may think I was manipulating my bosses, but my motives were pure with no personal gain or agenda. I was trying to make the place better. A former student perfectly framed this type of scenario several years ago: When you go to Spain, you speak Spanish to the extent possible. When you go to France, you speak French to the extent possible. This is no different. I was simply trying to speak their unique personality language to the extent possible. I was trying to meet people in their comfort zones.

In addition to everyday uses of the model, consider one of the most important communications people of influence and responsibility have—the crucial conversation. They are not fun; we often avoid them. Yet, they are a necessity at home, work, school, across nearly every aspect of human connectivity. Let's look at a crucial conversation at work using what we have learned from the DISC model.

* * * *

As a supervisor, Mary often needs to have conversations with her employees that can be very uncomfortable. This morning, Donna, one of her employees, walks into Mary's office and shuts the door.

Donna: I'm not sure how to say this, but Larry stinks.

Mary: What? I've always thought he was a hardworking and very nice person.

Donna: No, no, I'm not talking about his work. I mean . . .

he smells bad—like really bad—like all the time. You have to do something about it.

For a minute, Mary thought this would be a perfect time to work on her delegation skills. However, Mary knew Donna would not hear of that, and Donna would be right. This was part of Mary's job, not Donna's. Mary thanked Donna and sent her on her way. This is the first time (and hopefully the last) Mary has had to deal with hygiene issues with an employee.

From what Mary knows about the DISC model, she believes Larry is a C/D profile. Mary is an S/I. Mary waits an hour and then calls Larry to her office.

Mary: Good morning Larry, how have you been?

Larry: Good, and you?

Mary: Fine, fine…It's been a while since we've talked. How's the family?

Larry: Also good. Is there something on your mind? I'm really busy today.

Mary: Well, yes. Have you been experiencing any issues lately? Anything at home or with your coworkers?

Larry: No, I have not. Again, is there something on your mind?

Mary: Larry, well…this is not easy to say. It has come to my attention that you, uhm, may have some hygiene issues.

Larry: Hygiene issues…what exactly are you talking about… cutting my fingernails, ironing my clothes?

Mary: Larry, some of your coworkers have told me you don't smell good.

Larry: What? I don't smell good? Like body odor? Do you smell me right now?

Mary: Well, no . . .but . . . Larry, is there anything going on that would cause this? Maybe something as simple as not doing your laundry enough or working out in the morning but getting a shower later in the day or evening. Or maybe something more serious like an illness or medication you are taking?

Larry: I have no idea. Am I in violation of company policy?

Mary: Larry, I never considered looking for some specific policy. I would hope it is assumed that proper hygiene is necessary in a professional work environment as well as with our clients.

Larry: What's next with this?

Mary: Well, I hope what's next is that you will address your hygiene, and we never have this conversation again. I truly hope you will not hold a grudge against me or anyone else about this.

Larry: You said several people complained about me. Who? Are these people sitting right outside your office where I sit, or are they customers? Who complained on me without having the decency to talk with me first?

Mary: Larry, I understand you are offended by the accusation and feeling somewhat betrayed. I'm very sorry about that. I knew this was going to be an uncomfortable conversation. But who complained to me is unimportant. Please work on your hygiene and feel free to talk with me any time if I can help in any way.

* * * *

How did Mary do? Mary did some things right and some things wrong. The first thing she perhaps got wrong was assuming Donna was correct. Because Mary is all about people (S and I above the line), she trusted Donna's assessment without any other evidence. Mary jumped straight to a crucial, impactful conversation with nothing more than the accusation of a single coworker.

The overarching problem with Mary's approach to the conversation was that she spoke from her comfort zone, her DISC profile, as opposed to approaching it from Larry's comfort zone. Consider the back and forth in the opening of the conversation. Mary's S and I dimensions needed to establish a rapport and ease into the conversation.

However, neither the C nor D dimensions need that. Indeed, they detest small talk. The boss just called the employee into the office and shut the door. Larry wants immediate answers to why he is there, not small talk about family and the weather. Meeting Larry in his comfort zone, Mary should have dispensed with the small talk and gone straight to the point.

When Mary did begin the actual dialogue about smelling bad, she still eased into it by framing it around hygiene. Again, no specificity, which left Larry not only confused but agitated. The lesson here is that if you really want to irritate anyone, particularly a C/D profile, insinuation and innuendo are good tools. Mary did both in this case by insulting Larry in an indirect way.

Mary then jumped again to her comfort zone by asking if there was anything going on that would cause this . . . showering, illness, medication. Showing an interest in root causes is almost always a good thing. However, it is tricky business.

First, Mary did this too soon. They had not even established that he smelled bad. Larry appears in denial, and Mary even admitted she could not smell him. Second, Mary's inquiry got very personal. Asking about medical issues may be prohibited by Mary's company policies or even laws. Again, Mary's inquiry was well-intentioned. The S and I dimensions in her inform a need to help in any way possible. Yet, the C and D dimensions in Larry resent this inquiry into personal lives.

Larry asked if he had violated company policy. Mary didn't know, and she should have known. She had an hour before she called Larry to her office. She could have used that hour not only to think about how to approach a C/D employee with such a sensitive issue, but what the policies and rules are concerning hygiene. Surely a High C employee will want to know.

Larry asked Mary what comes next. While her answer was generally appropriate, she did not offer enough specificity for a C/D. Larry wanted a step-by-step process of what's next. Mary even added that she hoped he would not hold any grudges. Again, an appropriate comment in general but of little value to a C/D.

Larry wanted to know who went behind his back to complain. Mary handled that appropriately. She began to offer more clarity as the conversation progressed. In a nice way, she even pushed back on Larry by identifying his feelings and by not answering his question because it was irrelevant. She even ended the conversation in an appropriate way that a C/D would appreciate.

The following is a quick reference chart for what behaviors you may want to consider and employ when communicating with people who have different behavioral preferences than you.

Disc Profile	Your Behavior
High D	Be direct, to the point without focusing on details. Be firm but respectful. Display competence and honesty.
High I	Talk in the narrative. Display enthusiasm and energy. Be friendly, upbeat, and willing to engage.
High S	Relax your emotions. Show sincerity, warmth, and appreciation for their position. Avoid direct attacks.
High C	Prepare, know the facts, and speak clearly and concisely. Use evidence as opposed to an emotional argument.

Closing Thoughts

Learning about ourselves, how we perceive our external world, is of crucial importance. Yet, the value of the DISC model expands rapidly when we begin to understand and appreciate other's profiles - their needs, fears, motivations, and perceptions. The real value in the model is when we use this information to adapt our behavior to meet others in their comfort zone – when we look beyond behavior to the needs and motives behind other's behavior.

DISC offers a way for us to estimate another person's emotional and psychological needs so that we may take constructive, deliberate actions that increase our capacity to effectively connect and communicate with those around us. As we have discussed throughout the text, high Ds want autonomy, control, and new challenges. High I profiles tend to value recognition, social acceptance, and respect from others. High S profiles need appreciation for their hard work, safety, and support. High Cs appreciate precision, value, and quality. When we strive to view other people's behaviors through the lens of their needs rather than our own, we can begin to improve all aspects of human connectivity.

Moving Forward 10

The American Psychological Association (APA) defines perception as "the process or result of becoming aware of objects, relationships, and events by means of the senses, which includes such activities as recognizing, observing, and discriminating." We gather data through our senses and use our brains to make sense of that raw information. This interpretation is unique to each of us, which leads to different judgments and assumptions about our environment, the people around us, and ourselves. One person may perceive a dog jumping on them as dangerous, while another may perceive this action as an act of love or joy from the dog. Sometimes our interpretations are wrong due to a variety of biases, experiences, and self-deceptions we bring to the process. We meet someone for the first time who reminds us of someone we once knew. We may immediately ascribe our feelings of the long-ago acquaintance to this new person regardless of the accuracy. And the first impressions we make about people tend to last. In fact, first impressions are remarkably resistant to contrary information even if the contrary information is correct, and our original perceptions were faulty.

Most of the time our perceptions are not right or wrong, they are just different than what others perceive. We often pay selective attention to some aspects of the environment, particularly elements that are of interest to us. We equally ignore other elements of our environment that may be instantly apparent

> *Only a small portion of reality,
> for a human being, is what is
> going on; the greater part is
> what he or she imagines in
> connection with the sights and
> sounds of the moment.*
>
> *– Suzanne Langer*

to others. The unique nature and often flawed process of the perception process can lead to miscommunications and misinformed decisions and actions. For example, you give a task to several of your employees to complete. A few days later when the tasks are submitted, you see one product of your liking and expectations but three that make no sense to you. The varied results may be that the employees had varied perceptions of what you were asking of them.

People certainly have their own unique ways of perceiving and behaving that are often both identifiable and predictable. William Marston believed everyone behaves in all four DISC dimensions throughout their lives, constantly alternating depending on their perceptions of their environment and their power in relation to that environment. However, most people get comfortable in one or two styles and do not significantly change even in different situations. DISC is about one's comfort zone. It is not fixed, but it is often difficult for people to get out of their safe, secure, and accustomed way of behaving. Influential Irish writer Maria Edgeworth offered in the early 1800s, "The diminutive chains of habit are scarcely ever heavy enough to be felt, until they are too strong to be broken." It is up to each of us to recognize our chains in the formative stages and develop the necessary tools of flexibility and adaptability to alter our natural behaviors based on the needs of the situation and those around us.

I frequently ask my classes two questions that often stir quite a discussion. Are we defined by our choices? Considering so many internal and external contextual influences beating down on us every day (media, advocates, friends and family, our own experiences and personality, the exponential habits we have created over our lifetimes), do we even have the capacity to make our own decisions? Arguments can be made on both sides of these questions, but I believe we do have the power to choose, and those decisions define who we are. As Wayne Dyer observed, "Our lives are the sum total of the choices we have made."

From how much we exercise to how often we get a physical or go to the dentist to our purchasing habits to our commitment to life-long learning to the extent of our generosity and kindness to the kinds of jobs and careers we have, our entire lives represent a series of choices that dramatically influence our perceptions and decisions thus defining who we really are. We face choices everywhere all throughout the day, and every one of them has the potential to have a lasting impact on our lives.

To a large extent, our decisions are the product of our natural perceptions and subsequent responses to the world. A kind and supportive high S profile may be more inclined to put a dollar in a homeless man's cup but less inclined to confront the waiter who brought her a well-done steak after she ordered medium-rare. A high D profile may be more inclined to take charge of an unruly group of people but less inclined to listen intently and empathize with one of his employees struggling through stressful times. Yet, we never have to be prisoners of our perceptions and natural responses to the world. Each of us has the power to change how we perceive both our environment and our role in that environment.

Look at this picture. What do you immediately see?

Most of you initially will see water, rocks, perhaps a mountain. Now, turn your head 45 degrees to the left while looking at the picture. Do you see a woman and her child with their hands together at their chest as if they are praying? All you did was turn your head slightly to the left to reveal a profoundly different reality. Changing our perceptions is often difficult, but as illustrated by this simple example, it is not impossible.

Understanding perception and human behavior through the lens of the DISC model gives us tools for better communication and conflict management skills as well as increased tolerance and acceptance. But understanding is of no value without action and reflection. At best, action without reflection leads to uninformed responses to the world. At worst, it leads to reckless encounters with those around us. Reflection without action is just self-indulgence with no foreseeable end.

It is now up to you to take this new appreciation for the differences in each of our personalities and do something with it. Recognize our perceptions are partial and subjective. Ask clarifying questions of others and yourself and be open to answers that might go against your beliefs. Each of us has the power, the responsibility,

> *We cannot become what we need by remaining what we are.*
>
> *~ John C. Maxwell*

to alter our behavior towards the needs of the situation and people to whom our behavior impacts. Perception drives our behavior. We interpret our environment, create responses, and act accordingly. Change your perceptions, change your behavior.

SOURCES

Allessandra, T., & O'Connor, M. (1992). *People smart: Powerful techniques for turning every encounter into a mutual win*. La Jolla, CA: Keynote Publishing Company.

Anderson, R., & Carter, I. (1999). *Human behavior in the social environment: A social systems approach*. Hawthorne, NY: Aldine De Gruyter.

Bennis, W. (1989). *On becoming a leader*. Reading, MA: Addison-Wesley Publishing Company, p. 40.

Boss, J. (2015). www.forbes.com/sites/jeffboss/2015/03/20/how-to-overcome-the-analysis-paralysis-of-decision-making/#3265141c1be5

Brain Games- False Memory and Misinformation Effect. (2014, June). https://www.youtube.com/watch?v=qQ-96BLaKYQ

Buber, M. (1955). *Between man and man*. New York, NY: Macmillan.

Cicero, M. (2012). *On living and dying well*, Trans. Thomas Habinek, London, England: Penguin Books.

Cohen, M. www.macrobioticsinternational.com/site/assets/files/1069/macint_53_senses.pdf

Covey, S. (2013). *The 7 habits of highly effective people.* New York, NY: Rosetta Books.

Covey, S. M. (2006). *The speed of trust.* New York, NY: Free Press.

Dyer, W. https://awakenthegreatnesswithin.com/34-inspirational-wayne-dyer-quotes-to-change-your-mindset/

Einstein, A. www.washingtonpost.com/news/worlviews/wp/2017/10/24/einstein-scribbled-his-theory-of-happiness-in-place-of-a-tip-it-just-sold-for-more-than-1-million/?noredirect=on&utm_term=.42067080d7bf

Edgeworth, M. (1806). *Moral tales for young people.* Vol 1, London: Forester.

Favila, S., Kuhl, B., & Winawer, J. (2022). Perception and memory have distinct spatial tuning properties in human visual cortex. *Nature Communications, 13.*

Fromm, E. *Man for himself.* www.quoteland.com.

Gardner, J. (1990). *On leadership.* New York, NY: The Free Press.

Giles, L. (1988). *Sun Tzu on the art of war.* Graham Brash, Ltd, pp. 24-25.

Goleman, D. (1995). *Emotional intelligence.* New York, NY: Bantam Books.

Hall, C., Lindzey, G., & Campbell, J. (1998). *Theories of personality* (4th ed.). New York, NY: John Wiley & Sons, Inc.

Hersey, P., Blanchard, K., & Johnson, D. (2001). *Management of organizational behavior: Leading human resources* (8th ed). Upper Saddle River, NJ: Prentice-Hall, Inc.

Jung, C. www.brainyquote.com/authors/carl_jung

Knapton, S. (2016). www.telegraph.co.uk/news/science/science-news/12170295/Relationships-opposites-do-not-attract-scientists-prove.html

Leonard, M. (2018, May). www.universityofcalifornia.edu/news/yanny-vs-laurel-science

Marston, W. (1928). *The emotions of normal people.* New York, NY: Harcourt, Brace and Company.

Maxwell, J. https://www.goodreads.com/quotes/

Mehta, V. www.psychologytoday.com/us/blog/head-games/201412/do-opposites-really-attract-its-complicated

McLeod, S. A. (2018, October). *Fundamental attribution error. Simply Psychology.* www.simplypsychology.org/fundamental-attribution.html

Montoya, M. http://theconversation.com/no-opposites-do-not-attract-88839

Musashi, M. (1974). *A book of five rings,* Trans, Victor Harris, Woodstock, NY: The Overlook Press.

Nikolova, N. (2018). *Curious kids: Do different people see the same colours?*
> https://theconversation.com/curious-kids-do-different-people-see-the-same-colours-107972#:~:text=eye%20look%20different.-,Can%20we%20be%20sure%20that%20people%20see%20the%20same%20colour,just%20a%20tiny%20bit%20differently.

Paiget, J. (1952). *The origins of intelligence in children.* New York, NY: International Universities Press.

Personality tests are the astrology of the office. https://www.nytimes.com/2019/09/17/style/personality-tests-office.html

Proffitt, D. & Baer, D. (2020). Perception: How our bodies shape our minds. New York: St. Martin's Publishing Group.

Riecke, L. (2018, May). www.cnet.com/culture/yanny-laurel-leaves-scientists-as-mystified-as-we-are/

Ross, L. & Ward, A. (1996). Naive realism in everyday life: Implications for social conflict and misunderstanding. *Values and knowledge*, 103-135.

Seth, A. (2018). Anil Seth: How does your brain construct your conscious reality? TED Radio Hour. www.npr.org/transcripts/654730916

USS Montana v. Lighthouse. www.youtube.com/watch?v=NZ_ FOmMqXfE

Vander Zanden, J. (2003). *Human development* (7th ed.). New York: McGraw-Hill Companies, Inc.

Van Dyke, Henry. www.brainyquote.com/quotes/henry_van_ dyke_147311?src=t_personality

Wallisck, P. (April 2017). Two years later, we finally know why people saw "The Dress" differently. https://slate.com/ technology/2017/04/heres-why-people-saw-the-dress-differently.html#:~:text=Remember%2C%20 the%20dress%20is%20actually, Because%20shadows%20overrepresent%20blue%20light.differently. html#:~:text=Remember%2C%20the%20dress%20is%20 actually,Because%20shadows%20overrepresent%20 blue%20light.

Zigarmi, D., Blanchard, K., O'Connor, M., & Edeburn, C. (2004). *The leader within*. Upper Saddle River, NJ: Pearson Education Inc.

Jeffrey L. Green, Ph.D.

Dr. Green served as a police officer and FBI agent for over 30 years. During his tenure in the law enforcement community, he investigated and supervised investigations of criminal enterprises, ranging from white collar crimes to international drug trafficking to public corruption. For over ten years, he served at the FBI Academy in a variety of teaching and senior management positions. He was the Chief of Leadership Development and Chief of Faculty Affairs at the FBI Academy as well as the Faculty Coordinator for the University of Virginia National Academy Leadership Program.

Dr. Green served as an adjunct faculty member with the University of Virginia and Capella University. He founded the non-profit Center for Police Leadership & Ethics International (CPLE) in 2017 and currently serves as its President and CEO, teaching and building leadership programs for law enforcement leaders around the world.

Dr. Green earned B.S. and M.S. degrees in Criminal Justice Administration from Virginia Commonwealth University, and a Ph.D. in Criminal Justice from Capella University. Although his research efforts have focused primarily on the relationship between personality and leadership, he has published numerous articles on topics such as ethical leadership, leading change, human development, motivation and inspiration, contextual intelligence, and leading in a multicultural environment. He also is the author of *Graduate Savvy: Navigating the World of Online Higher Education* (in its 3rd edition), and *Decision Point: Real-Life Ethical Dilemmas in Law Enforcement* (in its 2nd edition).

Dr. Green can be reached at Jeff.Green@cpleinternational.org. For more information on our DISC courses, as well as a wide variety of leadership courses and programs, please visit us at www.cpleinternational.org.

Made in United States
Troutdale, OR
06/15/2024

20576525R00116